JOHN KNOWLI

The Life of the Yarmouth Naturalist Arthur Henry Patterson, A.L.S.

by

Beryl Tooley

Wilson-Poole Publishers
27 Greenborough Road
Sprowston
Norwich NR7 9HQ Tel 37402

First published October 1985

ISBN 0 9506592 7 4

Repro by APP (Origination) Limited, Norwich.
Printed and bound in the United Kingdom by Page Bros (Norwich) Ltd.

Acknowledgements

I am grateful to the following:

The County Archivist, Norfolk Record Office.
Lowestoft Central Library.
Great Yarmouth Central Library.
Great Yarmouth Naturalists' Society.
Dr. E. A. (Ted) Ellis, Wheatfen, Norfolk.
Mr. Percy Trett, Great Yarmouth, Norfolk
Mr. Brian Brown, Lowestoft, Suffolk.
Mr. Harold Jenner, St. Olaves, Norfolk.
Mr. Herbert Doig, Norwich (grandson of A. H. Patterson).
Miss Cecilia Patterson, Great Yarmouth, Norfolk
(Granddaughter of A. H. Patterson).
Mrs. Enid White, Caister, Norfolk (Granddaughter of A. H. Patterson).
Mrs. Monica Mobbs, Upton, Norfolk.
Mr. Jack Hacon, Manningtree, Essex.
Mr. Christopher Elliott, Wimbledon.
Mr. David Ferrow, Great Yarmouth, Norfolk.
Mrs. A. Smith, Caister, Great Yarmouth.
Miss Lavinia Wellicome, for the Marquess of Tavistock and the Trustees of the Bedford Estates.

To Mr. David Orr, Redgrave, Norfolk an especial thanks for reading the manuscript and my husband John for his patience and help.

Photographs

I am grateful to the following for permission to reprint photographs.

Norfolk Record Office (Manuscript No. follows photograph number) 5 (4181), 9 (4181), 10 (4202), 12 (4202), 13 (4181), 14 (4202), 15 (4202), 16 (4202), 17 (527), 25 (4209), 49 (4138), 54 (4138), 71 (4145), 72 (4150), 76 (4146), 78 (4150).

Norwich City Library Title Page, 22, 51, 56, 58, 64, 77.

Lowestoft Central Library 69, 73, 74.

By kind permission of the Marquess of Tavistock and the Trustees of the Bedford Estates 29, 30, 31.

Eastern Counties Newspapers, Norwich Mercury Series 67 (Eastern Daily Press), 82 (Yarmouth Mercury).

Mr. Percy Trett, 2, 3, 4, 8, 39, 57, 65, 68, 75, 80.

Mr. D. R. Nobbs 78 (Mss.4150 N.R.O.).

Mr. B. Ollington 1, 18.

Ford Jenkins (H. Jenkins Ltd.) 22, 66.

Mr. H. Jenner 60, 61.

Mr. B. Brown 37.

Photographs copied by John Tooley and processed by Brian Ollington, with exception of 6, 7, 34, 46 copied by John Mummery, 45 copied by Ford Jenkins, and 1 and 18 supplied by Brian Ollington.

Sources

Manuscripts and other material in the custody of Norfolk Record Office. References have been made to the following:

Notebooks 1878-1935, 44 volumes, Mss. 513-543, 4134-4146.

These volumes contain numerous records of A.H.Patterson's observations of the fauna, notes of curious and interesting specimens, pen and ink sketches and coloured drawings of interesting examples, letters from other naturalists, and numerous short articles and letters published in various periodicals and newspapers.

Some autobiographical reminiscences, 1916, vol. 1. Mss.4181
Personal reminiscences, photos, etc., 1916, vol. 1. Mss.4209.
Reminiscences of a Norfolk Naturalist, Mss. 4210.

Cook, F. Personal diaries in custody of Lowestoft Central Library.
Eastern Counties Newsapers, Ltd., Norwich Mercury Series.
Great Yarmouth Naturalists Society history by Mr. M. Bean.
Patterson, A. H., "Shadow Entertainments and How to Work them," 1895.
Patterson, A. H., "From Hayloft to Temple," 1903.
Patterson, A. H., "A Souvenir of 20 years work as a School Attendance Officer," 1912.
Patterson, A. H., "Through Broadland in a Breydon Punt," 1920.

Patterson, A. H., "Holiday Nights and Days on Breydon," 1921, Norwich Mercury Series.
Patterson, A. H., "The Cruise of the 'Walrus' on the Broads," 1923.
Patterson, A. H., "Wildfowlers and Poachers," 1929.
Rumbelow, P. Personal diaries by kind permission of Mr. P. Trett.
School Attendance Gazette, June 1902.
Smith, A. "The Broadland Naturalist" in Naturalists' Journal, Vol. 10, No. 114, 1901.
Weston, E. M. "John Knowlittle. Memories of Arthur Patterson the G.O.M. (Grand Old Man) of Norfolk Natural History" in The Field, November 9th, 1935.

Introduction

My great-grandfather, Arthur Henry Patterson, once said: "The lives of good, interesting and unique individuals never ought to pass away unnoticed into oblivion."

I grew up knowing very little about my great-grandfather. It was not until my fifth year at Yarmouth High School and my biology teacher invited the class to submit nature notebooks for a competition run by the Yarmouth Naturalists' Society, to win for the school the Arthur Patterson Shield, that I realised the importance of this ancestor of mine.

Eight years ago his books were becoming increasingly rare, but I set about collecting them and they formed the nucleus of an interest in the great-grandfather I never knew. When my father died two years ago I came across some family photographs, mostly undated, and they set me thinking more about Arthur Patterson and gave me the idea of writing this book.

There is considerable interest in Arthur Patterson "memorabilia" amongst naturalists in East Anglia today and they have supported and encouraged me along the way. In particular I would like to mention three—Dr. E. A. (Ted) Ellis, Mr. Percy Trett and Mr. Brian Brown. To them I am immensely grateful. My husband John patiently copied most of the photographs for the book and has been long-suffering when, at times, "A.P. appeared to take over my life!"

I have in the past two years read my great-grandfather's nature diaries, notebooks, autobiography, his published books and all the pamphlets and literature I could lay my hands on. I have talked to people who knew him and read personal diaries of his contempories. I shall never forget the words of advice from Ted Ellis: "Read the diaries, all of them . . . your problem will be 'trying to see the wood for the trees.' "

In October 1985 we celebrate the 50th anniversary of Arthur Patterson's death and this biography, which I dedicate to my father, Howard Patterson Saunders who, like his grandfather, was a "good, interesting and unique individual" ensures neither "will pass away unnoticed into oblivion."

Beryl G. Tooley
January 1985

Contents

Foreword

I was fortunate enough to enjoy the companionship of Arthur Patterson in the last thirteen years of his life, on long walks in the country around Great Yarmouth, on his beloved Breydon Water and the Broads, and in the intimacy of his study as he scribbled articles, books and lively pen-and-ink sketches or was joined on a winter's evening by a coterie of naturalist friends. Sometimes I accompanied him when he gave talks, illustrated by humorous lightning sketches, in village halls and schools, and as he threaded the streets of Yarmouth or Norwich, calling on numerous acquaintances, among them some of the old Breydoners who figured in his published reminiscences. We would call at Yarmouth fish-wharf on the chance of collecting rare specimens saved for his inspection, or stroll down to a beach where draw-netters were hauling in their catch. His sprightliness and sense of the comical ensured a welcome wherever he went. There was the salt of the sea in the mellow timbre of his voice, which echoed the dialectical blend special to his native town. He looked about like a Sir Thomas Browne, seeking new wonders and delving into mysteries with the eagerness of a child of the Renaissance. His articles and major works on local natural history were often characterised by a raciness and air of adventure. In perfecting his word-craft and style over the years I know that he derived inspiration from favourite authors such as Defoe, R.L.Stevenson and Thoreau. His honesty was unswerving, although he held strong opinions apt to be considered eccentric on occasion. Though, as is only too clear in this biography, he had to battle against odds which might have been expected to sour the temperament of the most patient of men, he rose to every occasion with a blithe spirit. In working his passage as a recorder of Nature and humanity, he never aspired to academic stature, but nevertheless, by his warmth of purpose, astute observation and commonsense, succeeded in communicating his interest and enthusiasm to others in a meaningful and sympathetic way. While triumphing in discovery, he was not boastful, regarding arrogance as a badge of charlatans.

At the age of seventeen I typed "Wildfowlers and Poachers" at his dictation from the rough manuscript, discussing it, sentence by sentence, in the bond of true friendship. He had many young disciples who sought guidance from near and far and how generous he was in encouraging them! His advice for aspiring writers was simple: "Start writing and what is in your mind will flow out with the ink like a spring out of the ground; be sparing with adjectives and keep something in the locker for another time."

Fifty years after his death, it gives me great pleasure to contribute this brief foreword to a well-researched account of his life by one of his great grand-daughters, in whose eyes, from time to time, I catch a glimpse of my old hero.

Ted Ellis

Chapter I

The Breydoners

> "I wedged in amongst them in the late 'sixties . . . they looked upon me as a camp follower and somewhat of an enigma . . . I pocketed a notebook and filled the pages of Breydonlore and anecdotes, gleaning up what to them were commonplace."
>
> A. H. PATTERSON

On a foggy November afternoon in 1870 Arthur Patterson made his first acquaintance with the Breydoners. He was thirteen years old and accompanied a newsboy chum delivering the weekly local newspaper to John Bessey, landlord of the Bowling Green public house by Breydon Water. It was a busy and prosperous establishment.

The landlord, a typical East Anglian with "rubicund face, keen blue eyes and a snowy beard," was, like his customers, a colourful character. He was a punt-gunner and eel-merchant, said to be "as exact with his ale-measures as he was with his beam-scale." The pub was within sight and sound of Breydon Water, the tidal estuary of the River Yare—a remnant of the great estuary Gariensis Ostium that swept up to Norwich in Roman times. Four and a half miles long and three-quarters of a mile wide in some parts its vast expanse of mud-flats covered and left bare by every tide attracted almost every species of wildfowl and wader that frequented the British shores.

Many years later Arthur recalled the day in his book "Wildfowlers and Poachers".

"The creaking of the tavern signboard added to the witchery of the gathering shadows . . . voicing—eerily—a welcome . . . There was, too, a club-like air about the place, where men of kindred occupations and tastes could discuss, over mugs and pewters their mutual rivalries and reminiscences.

"My heedful boyish mind was instantly impressed by the sawdust-smothered floor, it smelt *so* like a circus. Dotted about were dust-filled spittoons; there were stuffed birds on the shelves behind the counter in an odd setting of barrels and bottles . . . The centre of comfort was the old iron stove, with its glowing red body, whose blackleaded chimney-pipe poked a way out through the wall . . .

". . . the lounging smokers on the worn settles, some arguing guns and prowess with rough unmusical voices; others as silent and meditative, yet alert to pick up advantageous gossip, with lips focused into pouting rings, like touched sea-anemones, into which short clay pipes had been thrust. The faces of the men, lined and hardened by storm and sun, were full of character, indexing a sturdy, contentious self-reliance . . ."

A bowling green had existed there since the 17th century and had provided a source of amusement and recreation to many an old eel-catcher and wildfowler

1 Looking up Breydon from the "Bowling Green"

2 A game of bowls at the "Bowling Green" tavern. From P.H. Emerson's "Wildlife on a Tidal Water"

who indulged with propriety on this very harmless exercise. Well-trampled, it ran down to a parapet at the waterside where the men could lean and gossip and watch the wherries, laden with merchandise, sail by up Breydon, and enjoy a drink and a pipe of baccy. Tall elms ran around the three sides of the square green leaving the water view free and unshaded. On either side stood rough boatsheds, boat-builders' workshops and warehouses, and landing-stages and rollered slopes where the Breydoners moored or hauled out their punts.

Breydon was the haunt of an interesting race of men. During the first half of the 19th century it was an eel-man's "Paradise", a punt-gunner's "Promised Land." The Breydoners were hardy, grim, observant, self-contained illiterate toilers—many of them lacking any ambition save to earn their daily bread. There was freedom, independence and variety in the wildlife of the waters of the estuary and their lives were a mixture of serious quest and sport.

With no harbour dues to pay, the wildfowler and smelter could moor his houseboat wherever he chose without obstruction, and tether his punt to the quayside without an anxious thought beyond fear of meddlesome urchins, who were, unconsciously, becoming initiated into the self-same occupation as their elders. Breydon house-boats or "Noah's Arks" as they were called differed little

3 A typical "Noah's Ark" on Breydon Water. From P.H. Emerson's "Wildlife on a Tidal Water"

externally, and were simply huts with nearly flat roofs, or were built span-roof fashion on a condemned, but not necessarily worn-out, smacksboat. Only in internal arrangements did they differ.

Stoves warmed the cabins, lockers usually filled up the ends fore and aft, and settles served as cupboards below. The Breydoner bundled in his houseboat nets and much of his gear, and he slept soundly upon a sack thrown over the nets and corks, with another sack or a blanket flung over himself. Outside floated his eel-trunks—a wooden equivalent of a "keep-net"; on the roof you would find his poles, eel-picks and sails. He was a Robinson Crusoe afloat.

The Breydoners had a hard life—as did their women and children. Their living was ruled by the tides and seasons. On wintry days a wildfowler went off in pursuit of wigeon, mallard, pochard and waders in the "greys" of winter. In the spring, he pursued godwit, knot and migrant flocks of "smee" (wigeon). Spoonbills were hoped for in the summer, while "gentleman-gunners" and collectors sought his help to secure sandpipers and desirable visitors. On summer nights he babbed for eels until morning; netted for "butts" (flounders) for crab-men; mullet for fishmongers; and, when smelts abounded, changed his nets for their encapture.

At intervals a Breydoner took a short spell ashore to lay in store of shot, powder, edibles and water, and put on a much needed change of under-garments—his outer garments he never appeared to change, nor replenish, for they were made curiously durable by ooze, eel-slime, and the blood of slaughtered fowl. He talked of little else but the ways and doings of wildfowl and waders, and of the habits and idiosyncracies of eels, and smelts, and mullet. Breydon was his World.

Arthur's father rented an allotment just a stone's throw away from Breydon on the Runham marshes. As a small boy, perched on a barrow load of horse manure, "like a king on a golden throne" he accompanied him to the allotment. The place was like "Paradise" and there he developed his fertive love of nature. There were rabbits and bantams to feed and pet, or wood-lice, caterpillars and beetles to find. In the ditch that bordered the allotment, he studied the habits of Ditch prawns (Paloemon varians) and chased dragonflies as they flitted among the nodding reed-tops.

The lure of Breydon was strong. He found if he climbed onto the roof of the little shed, he could see beyond the railway the "walls"—zigzagging mounds that had been thrown up above the level of high water when the dykes were dug to drain the "saltings." He could see a streak of silver water, and he wondered about the queer cries and pipings coming from there and the crack of punt guns.

On Fridays, Police Sergeant Barnes went into Arthur's stepmother's shop in Charlotte Street (Howard Street) to buy his weekly supply of tobacco. The boy looked forward to these visits. As he listened to the week's police gossip, he thought the activities of the poachers and wildfowlers were like the "Songs of Solomon."

Chapter II

Humble Beginnings

"Plod will make a naturalist who gets enough time; genius for the wild is only an accident of birth or environment."
A. H. PATTERSON

Arthur's great-grandfather was a Scottish highlander. He became a soldier and fought under General Wolfe at Quebec in 1758. Unscathed he came home from the war and settled in Norfolk at King's Lynn and later moved to Norwich to work as a pavior, paving the streets of Norwich. It was said when he died Norwich City owed him £100. He was placed in his coffin with a parcel of snuff and his favourite drinks.

His son James became a shoemaker and traded in Lower Westwick Street and on Castle Meadow (where Anglia Television stands today). He was a staunch Methodist and was credited with being one of the first instigators in Norwich to fight against church rates, remaining so in spite of being elected a churchwarden.

Arthur's father, William Patterson, was born on December 18th, 1818 in Magdalen Street, Norwich. He worked as a shoe-overlooker in a Norwich factory, and, like his father, was a staunch Methodist and taught in the New City Sunday School and the Lady Jane Wesleyan School.

Hoping to "better himself" in 1845 he and his pretty fair-haired wife Mary Ann moved to Great Yarmouth. They set up home in the "Rows" where William cobbled shoes and, to make ends meet, Mary helped with the "sew-rounding".

Yarmouth was built on the sandbank which gradually formed at the mouth of the estuary Gariensis Ostium. Herring abounded in the surrounding seas and with fishermen coming from near and far, Yarmouth became an important seafaring town. In 1260 Henry III granted permission for the town to be enclosed by a defensive wall and moat. It took 100 years to complete the wall because of the Black Death. Due to a shortage of local building stone, the walls and towers were built of local flints and pebbles lying on the beaches and in the immediate neighbourhood. Parts of the wall remain to this day.

The town wall not only kept out invaders, it determined the shape and size of the town for many centuries. No-one was permitted to live outside the walls and the small area within made it necessary for the houses to be built as closely as possible. By building in parallel lines more could be accommodated and thus the "Rows" were born.

The "Rows", probably a corruption of the French *rue* meaning "a street", were unique in England. Originally numbering 145, many were destroyed completely in the Second World War while others were later pulled down for new development. In Arthur's time the Rows were chiefly inhabited by persons in the humbler walks of life, or occupied as fish-houses, store-rooms and malt-houses. The Rows provided easy access to all parts of the town. There was a natural fall of

4 A typical Yarmouth Row from P.H. Emerson's "Wildlife on a Tidal Water"

land between the Market Place and the Quay, so rainwater drained away quickly down the Rows and a current of air rid the streets of the smoke-filled stale atmosphere.

The houses were built very close together. The streets were roughly made with broken flints brought up from the beach, which made walking difficult and uncomfortable. Because of the narrowness of the Rows (sometimes just 3 ft. wide) "troll-carts" were used to carry herring and other merchandise from one end of the town to the other. The carts were about 12 ft. long and just over 3 ft. wide, with a very short, low back axle with wheels running under the body of the carriage. They were easy to load and when not in use took up little space when tipped on end with the shafts in the air.

Life was hard in the Yarmouth Rows. Waste was thrown into open gutters in the streets to run down to the drains on the quay and, as a result of the poor sanitary conditions, fevers and dysentery were commonplace. Water was obtained from one of numerous communal pumps in the streets.

5 Birthplace of Arthur Patterson, Row 36 or ''Garden Row'' so-called because of the quaint little garden plots in front of half a dozen of the houses. The gable end in the centre is that of number 9. He was born in number 8

My great-grandfather was born on October 19th, 1857 at No. 8, Row 36 or ''Garden Row'' so named because some half-dozen of the houses had little gardens in front of them. Although registered at birth as Henry Arthur, he became known as Arthur Henry Patterson. He was, he described himself later in life ''the runt of the litter,'' and was the last child Mary Patterson bore. She suffered from consumption (probably tuberculosis) and when the doctor visited her in the last few months of her life, Arthur hid because he was so frightened of him.

Arthur was three when, wearied by many births and little income, his mother died in 1860. All the children were frail, like their mother, and Arthur was the only one to succeed in surviving the age of twenty-one. When he became of age, his father wrote down the names and dates of birth of his brothers and sisters. The document is pasted in Arthur's autobiography.

Eliza Letitia	born	October 24th 1840
Henry Ezekiel	born	August 5th 1842

Harriet	born	September 25th 1844
Mary Ann	born	April 2nd 1846
Matilda	born	January 2nd 1848
William	born	January 31st 1849
Henry	born	September 1853
Arthur Henry	born	October 19th 1857

6 The Patterson family on the beach just before his mother's death. Arthur is seated on his father's knee with William and Mary

William and Mary were the only brother and sister he remembered. It was Mary, he recollected, who lifted him onto her shoulders so that he could see the Eastern Counties Volunteers in their "pepper and salt uniforms" marching down

George Street to the sound of drums. Everyone had turned out to cheer and hear the old war song ditties:

> "For the captain with his whiskers,
> Took a shy glance at me,
> Took a shy glance at me,
> For the captain with his whiskers,
> Took a shy glance at me."

Arthur was barely five, but he never forgot the spectacle and the loyalty of the people. He wrote about this event much later in life but did not say what the occasion was. There was a Militia Depot on the south denes and I have found reference to Volunteer Corps drilling on the Denes on Good Friday 1860 when from 8,000 to 10,000 spectators turned out to watch. It may have been a similar event.

William Patterson took the deaths of his wife and children very philosophically and outwardly calmly, though he must have felt their loss acutely. Looking back, Arthur was convinced that, if their surroundings had been more airy and food more nutritious, probably all his brothers and sisters would have survived. He could not understand why his father did not get out of the house.

William Patterson did not believe in medicine and looked upon diseases and distresses as "sent of the Lord for chastisement, correction and edification." He abominated anything not mentioned in the Old Testament and his favourite reading was "The History of the Jews" and "God's Judgement." He loved the church and his Bible; his life was a kind of religious travail.

Soon after Mary died William remarried the strapping widow of a Naval man and the family moved from the small cottage in the Rows to Charlotte Street where the new Mrs. Patterson kept a little General Shop. He gave up shoemaking and became an Assurance Agent for the "Prudential". With a little extra money coming in, family life improved.

Chapter III

The Young Methodist

"From Hayloft to Temple." . . . A. H. PATTERSON

A hayloft above a stable on Hog Hill (Priory Plain) was the first home of the Yarmouth Primitive Methodist Circuit. Arthur's stepmother remembered the old hayloft days and the men and women who worshipped there. One of the quaint old hymns she sang went as follows:

> "Well, I'll be one among you, so here's my heart and hand;
> Henceforth I am a Primitive, one of your happy band;
> I love your modes of worship, I love simplicity,
> Farewell my old companions, a Primitive I'll be.
>
> Sing glory, hallelujah, the Lord is with us still.
> The little crowd increases that arose upon Mow Hill."
>
> From a grand old mission hymn.

In 1827 Samuel Atterby set about collecting subscriptions towards erection of a more suitable place of worship, and a Tabernacle was built two years later on the site of the old Hayloft. This was enlarged in 1850 and became the centre of a Circuit which extended fifteen miles from Yarmouth with devoted local preachers walking to the outlying villages to hold meetings.

When Arthur's father moved to Yarmouth he joined the Primitive Methodist Tabernacle and filled various subordinate offices, including that of Sunday School teacher. He and another devoted teacher named David Coe canvassed for scholars, picking up any little ragamuffin or stray urchin they could persuade to follow them, until, in one year, they had added one hundred children to the register. William Patterson taught for 26 years. During the '60's and '70's he conducted, with Henry Blyth and others in Yarmouth, a series of popular penny readings and temperance meetings.

At Chapel the Pattersons occupied one of the "free seats" and sat in a series running from father to the shortest of them "like steps". The smallest one usually monopolised Father's knee. Arthur described the seats much later in his book "From Hayloft to Temple."

"These free seats were simply deals 7″ × 3″ on which you had to sit fair and square and remain awake or lose your equilibrium. There were no backs to them and they were placed diagonally in order to help folks face the preacher. One end slipped into the wall; the other was supported by a short length of deal morticed into it, and at the other end morticed into a plank in the floor. A post kept the middle from sagging." Arthur remembered "how smooth and shiny and discoloured they were by age and hard work; for they were well used

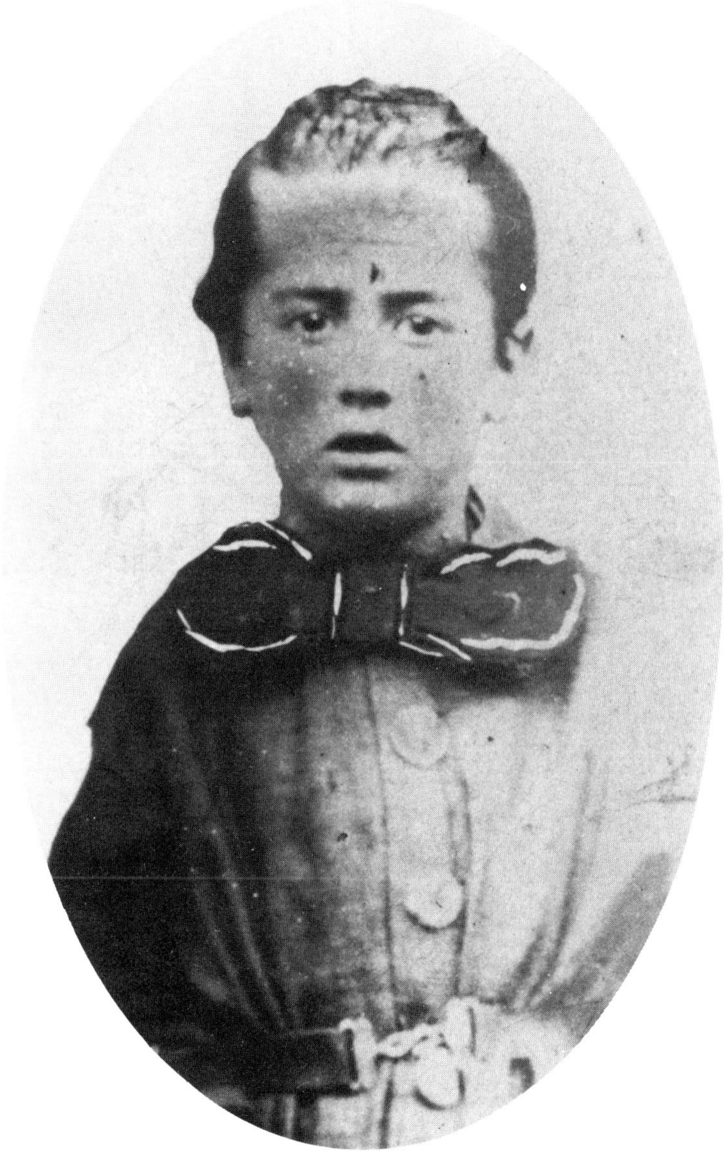

7 Taken from a "glass likeness" at the age of 7

and the poor gladly appropriated them. But for all that, those free seats were terrible back-achers . . ."

The Primitives understood the extreme importance of training the young and nurturing them in the ways of religion. Week by week, Arthur was taken to Chapel, and unconsciously it grew to be part of the routine of his young life. Sunday was spent as follows:

8 a.m.	Morning Prayer Meeting
9.30 a.m.	Sunday School
10.30 a.m.	Transferred to Chapel for Sermon
2.30 p.m.	Sunday School
6 p.m.	Preliminary Prayer Meeting
6.30 p.m.	Service at Chapel
8-9 p.m.	Prayer Meeting

He passed through every class in Sunday School from bottom to top, then began them again in the capacity of Sunday School Teacher. Of the hardworking staff of teachers, Arthur's favourite was Mr. Pigney, whose gentle, persuasive manner made the boy desire to be good. The "Book of Job" was Arthur's favourite book in the Bible, and he often lost his turn reading a verse because he was jotting down in pencil on the blank fly sheet at the end all the birds and animals mentioned.

It was a cramped upbringing for a boy who was "rattling with mirth and loved life and all things with enthusiasm." Sunday School Treats (outings) were a special delight, when sports were held on the North Denes and the following day, the scholars—sometimes numbering 500—and teachers marched, proudly, round the town.

Arthur's stepmother was known as "Sister Jane" at Chapel. She was a red-hot Methodist and proud to call herself a "ranter." She doted on Camp Meetings and took Arthur with her, far afield on hired coal-carts, or they walked to Caister or to Skinner's Piece, by the flour mill, on the Denes. The Denes was a well known haunt of migratory birds. The long stretch of marram hills was covered with great gorse bushes, whose bright yellow flowers made the whole scene gay and the north-east winds carried their delightful scent into the town. The place was alive with birds—hedge-sparrows and linnets, wheatears and redbacked shrikes whose half-eaten victims in the shape of field-mice and other creatures, were stuck here and there on thorns. Woodpigeons, turtledoves and stockdoves sought the seeds of various dene plants. Underfoot bright yellow Biting Stonecrop (Sedum acre) grew in great profusion and it was the first wild flower to take his eye.

When the sermons at Camp Meetings became boring and the pious congregation groaned and ranted, the boy organised grasshopper hunts with the other children, much to the displeasure of his parents. They were utterly unsympathetic to his childhood love of nature and lectured him often. To try and solemnize the boy's mind he was taken to the churchyard.

Instead of meditating amongst the tombstones, he preferred to hunt amongst the long grass round the graves for beetles and birds' nests, and gaze skywards at the angular flights of gulls going seawards or towards Breydon.

On Sunday, December 6th, 1874, a Trust was set up, with William Patterson as

8 Primitive Methodist Temple and Day School, Gt. Yarmouth

one of the trustees. The Primitive congregation had become large and ambitious, and it was proposed the Tabernacle be replaced by a Temple. Arthur was working as a Pupil Teacher at the Day School next door and was able to watch the Temple being built. He gave the workmen 4d.—which they spent on beer—to lay one of the first half-dozen bricks laid in for the foundation on the south front corner. For the plain living Methodists whose roots began in a hayloft, the Temple, seating one thousand people, with its lofty, classical front, was a remarkably imposing building.

9 Arthur's father William Patterson and stepmother in their seventies. Ann was William's second wife, his third marriage took place at the age of 81 and he yearned for another matrimonial venture at the age of 90!

Chapter IV

Schooldays

"I am glad I came last, for in my observation upon men, I have noticed that it is usually the youngest son who strikes out a line for himself—whilst the eldest is prone to be content for others to do it for him."
A. H. PATTERSON

"My father" wrote Arthur in his autobiography, "was upright as a palm tree and in his notions narrow as a lath."

He abstained from drink from the age of fourteen, he did not swear, nor did he lie. He seldom laughed and if compelled to—the laugh went almost unnoticed, and joking was certainly out of the question. He did not believe in any kind of sport, hated the gun, and wouldn't hurt a fly. He left his bantams to die of old age!

After his father remarried Arthur was taken to have his curls shorn, and, when he refused to say "Good Morning" to the barber, was carted snivelling and kicking to an Old Dame's School in the Glass House Row, where an old lady for one farthing a day cared for young children. The small warren of mites scratched slates and learned nothing but envy the old girl's toffees and sweets that filled her bottles, and which she occasionally gave to those from whom she could confiscate farthings. The school was a storage place for kiddies like Arthur from the Rows, when their mothers went charring or worked in the factories and fish-houses.

When not at school Arthur's playmates were the cats that swarmed in the Rows, and he amused himself making toys out of sticks and paper and sailing paper boats down the gutters to the outside drains. His stepmother was rough and uncultivated, but she fed him well and ruled vigorously. She was sharp-tempered and a strict disciplinarian, and her fat warm hand had a sting in it. His father, he remembered, went missing at punishment time, and never once in his life laid a finger on him. His word was Law!

Stepmother kept a grey parrot called "Polly" who had learned sailor language coming from Africa in the fo'c'sle. Polly sung snatches of Methodist ditties and often the pious and vulgar phases became mixed up! She fussed over her mistress and regurgitated food (as parrots do) to try and feed her, and she bit young Arthur like an alligator, given the chance.

Arthur spent his schooldays at the Primitive Methodist threepenny Day School on Hog Hill. His teacher, William Wallis, was a small, active man, "all nerves and go," but kindly and sympathetic. He came from Wiltshire to a school that was badly equipped and the few books available for the children were Irish readers. Many of the slates were broken and some had no frames.

Wallis rubbed into Arthur a tolerable knowledge of reading and writing and encouraged composition, music and song. The children sung lustily to his baton—which also stung their buttocks of:

10 Arthur at the age of 10 with "Polly" the grey parrot. He wrote of this photograph: "I was clad in breeches by my stepmother who was not a very artistic tailoress"

"Violets, violets, beautiful blue violets,
Laden with perfume, and dripping all with dew,
From dell and from dingle, by rill and rivulet,
Lady, at sunrise, I sought them for you!"

Arthur was corner-man tenor, until his voice broke. After that his efforts at singing were described as "like those of a duck swallowing hot potatoes." The only instrument the boy ever mastered was the comb-and-tissuepaper. He was a poor student of arithmetic and money problems.

Wallis taught drawing on two afternoons a week by classes—a pattern was drawn on the board which the children copied. Arthur drew well. Friday was "leisure day" and when wet, standing on a stool to reach the blackboard, he amused the other kiddies by doing sketches for them. On fine Friday afternoons Wallis took the children on nature rambles to the North Denes, to Mautby across the marshes, or to Burgh Castle. He taught Arthur to love the countryside and the wild flowers of which he was passionately fond.

The first bird Arthur handled was a sparrow which had been trapped and forgotten by some boy in a brick-trap in the churchyard. He and a chum discovered it on the way home from Sunday School.

"Let the poor thing go," said Arthur.

"No." the other replied.

They argued the point and Arthur won.

When he had saved up 2d. he bought his first nature book—"Gleanings from Natural History." Its twenty-odd pages swarmed with elephants, owls, crocodiles and other creatures, and he soon knew every line by heart and wished his stepmother might substitute such volumes for the Psalms.

"The contents of the book," he wrote, "ate into me like a fever and gave me a passion for nature."

Later he received as a birthday present Reverend Houghton's "Seaside Walks of a Naturalist," which encouraged an interest in fish, draw-nets, and so on. His third book was one on American birds. His favourite chapter in it was one on Water Rail shooting, and although it was to be a long time before he possessed a gun, he maintained the book "made a Sportsman of me".

As soon as he knew his way to the riverside, he was after crabs among the seaweeds at the tide-mark, and from the dykes he collected newts, sticklebacks and water snails which he took home in empty pickle bottles. His stepmother "abhorred his muddy clothes and very energetically dusted his jacket." She cursed the various "pets" he kept. Amongst them were silkworms and bumble bees, rats and white mice, hedgehogs, guinea pigs and a tortoise. Having nowhere to keep the tortoise, he placed it in a drawer used for his father's clean collars and laundry. Going to the drawer one day to take out a shirt-front, out popped the tortoise's innocent little head to the old girl's horror. She fled, thinking it was a snake!

In spite of everything, she really like the boy. She bought him "Chatterbox" a comic in which were interesting articles about birds and animals, and she took him to the menageries and the circus when they came to Town. In return, Arthur helped his stepmother in the shop, serving ha'p'orths of tea, penn'orths of butter, and snuff, or, sorting potatoes in the cellar. He collected black sausages from the smoker at the end of Middlegate Street, candles from Tunbridges and ran errands. He enjoyed visiting the common lodging houses in the Rows, and made friends with the "Cockney Bills", the beggars, minstrels and peg-makers.

Like most boys, Arthur started a collection of birds' eggs. However, he had scruples about taking eggs from the nest, so he gave marbles or ha'pence to those boys who would. He wanted to learn about the creatures he came across. The few books he had did not contain the information he wanted, so he talked to the bird-catchers and fisherfolk, but they used provincialisms. One told him a dunlin was a "stint", another a ringed plover was a "dottrell." A crow was a "spring rook", a goldfinch a "King Harry" or "Draw-water", and a yellowhammer was a "guler." As for smaller fry—crustacea, insects, and such like who knew or cared what they were called?

When he was 15 Arthur was appointed Pupil Teacher under Wallis at the Day School for five shillings a week. He was a good disciplinarian and in many cases found sketching things on the blackboard for the children was an easier method of explanation than verbal description. When the School Board came into existence the Day School was closed and he then taught for a while at the Trafalgar Road Board School.

Chapter V

The Gunner

> "In those early days of the 'close season' I was a sad, sad sinner. Often did a watcher lay in wait for me". A. H. PATTERSON

After four years teaching, Arthur began to suffer with chest trouble and, knowing of his family history, became increasingly worried about tuberculosis. When offered a job by Bartlett, the Superintendent of Regents Park Zoological Gardens, the doctor advised against his taking the job because of the London atmosphere.

At about this time Arthur became acquainted with a Breydoner named Benjamin Harwood. He was then in his thirties, a shoemaker by profession, student of the classics, and was a Primitive Methodist lay preacher. Arthur wrote of him:

> "My beloved spake and said unto me—rise up . . . and come away . . . the time of the singing of birds is come and the voice of the turtle (dove) is in our land." (The Song of Solomon, ch. 2)

Ben became his Breydonian mentor, and, as he wrote later in life "made a Naturalist and Broadländer of me." He took him on his first trip on Breydon in his handbuilt punt and Arthur never forgot "the exhilaration of the sail, the passing of much-surprised curlews feeding on the end of a drain, and the wildness of the flats at half-ebb tide." Ben taught him how to handle a punt, catch eels, use a butt-net ("butt" is the local name for flounder), a bird-net, catch shrimps and cure herrings in his old smokehouse.

Ben, like all the Breydoners, made a habit of leaving his gun loaded under the forepeak of the punt. One day Ben's son, Bernie, took Arthur out in his father's punt and Arthur took a shot at a herring gull. The gun went off and sent him backwards in the punt, feet upwards fortunately, into the well of the boat. It was his first shot with a gun.

Arthur had a cousin Charles who was keen on shooting and gun-punting and with whom he enjoyed early morning jaunts. They devised a system whereby Charles pulled a piece of string hanging from Arthur's bedroom window that operated a bell near his bed to awaken him, or he threw pellets at the window.

When he managed to slip out of the house undetected, he pulled his togs on in the backyard while the old folk snored, but sometimes a creaking stair tread gave the game away and he was ordered back to bed. His father detested secrecy and Arthur knew if he asked permission, it would have been denied and he worried if Arthur was out an hour after "regulation hours."

After leaving schoolwork, at the age of 18, Arthur became an Assurance Agent for the "Prudential" taking on part of his father's "Book". At that time an agent's life was not a good catch; there was always a "balance" to keep juggling. Arthur did not enjoy the work, but he earned 17/- a week without "new business" premiums and he could follow his outdoor pursuits. He had some leisure time, and with plenty of open air work, his health improved and rambling and rowing toughened his constitution. His father was never able to fathom out his son's need for "idling about" as he called it.

Winds, tides, weather and migration ruled Arthur's direction, whether he went to beach, river walls or the Breydon marshes. He watched the birds, often with evil intent, but in striving to outwit and over-reach them he picked up, unconsciously, much about their habits and ways; and, in so doing, came across many a strange insect or fish. His earliest ambition was to write a book on Yarmouth birds.

Early one May morning, when out on Breydon, he fastened his punt to an old hulk on Breydon to take a look at waders using the mudflats as halfway house on their spring migration. He climbed aboard the old ship and lay in the sunshine. Presently a swallow, then another, flew out of the open hatch, and going in, he discovered a nest. There, in the middle of the vast estuary, the swallows brought off their young.

When Arthur saw a letter in "The Standard" from a gentleman who expressed surprise at seeing a kingfisher in the very heart of London, he was prompted to reply. On September 19th, just before his 21st birthday, his first contribution to the Press appeared in that paper. He spoke of the number of kingfishers that could be seen on Yarmouth denes, and accounted the story of the swallows' nest he observed on Breydon. Seeing his name in print was a new experience and he so cherished his first contribution that he obtained a "notebook" and pasted it therein. The letter was to be the forerunner of many hundreds of newspaper articles. In the same year Arthur began jotting down observations in his nature notebook after J. H. Gurney, F.L.S., F.Z.S., the naturalist, pointed out to him the importance of dating all incidents and records. Arthur Patterson was to write 44 diaries in the course of his lifetime and they are now in the custody of the Norfolk Record Office.

Arthur canvassed for the "Prudential" until July 1879, when he put on a postman's uniform and "learned the postman's knock." The job was a seasonal one, so, at the end of the summer, he obtained a Pedlar's Licence and peddled tea. "Profits," he wrote, "kept the wolf from the door", and an evening job at the Y.M.C.A. and the odd shilling for stuffed nature specimens sold to collectors made his weekly wage up to £1.0.0d.

Arthur's first attempt at taxidermy was a bird that turned out to be "a scarecrow—illshapen, lank and gaunt." His father thought it looked a picture and said: "If you could learn THAT and stick to it, you might produce a serious income—though I would prefer you to BUY the specimens, not SHOOT them."

Any spare hours were spent stuffing birds, weasels, squirrels—anything he could lay his hands on that was suitable. He made cases out of wood from grocer's boxes and collected grasses, lichens, twigs and mosses on his nature rambles. He enjoyed "boxing up" the specimens as it drew out his artistic feeling! Whilst he did not feel competent enough to take work in, he was able to sell it, and the profits he made bought books he needed, like Sir Jonathan Couch's "British Fishes." With those four volumes on his bookshelf, he felt a great man!

Several years earlier, at the age of seventeen, he had scraped together 16/- and bought an old muzzle gun from Manthorpe, "a notable woodcock shot", and Arthur became a shore-gunner. Knowing of his father's hatred of the gun—even more than of the Devil—he was afraid to take it home.

For a few years the Pattersons lived on Caister Road. There lived in the neighbourhood, a young man named Benjamin Dye, who worked in a bake-house. He was the same age as Arthur, was a skilled taxidermist and a gunner. They met one day when out on the denes, became partners and went out gunning regularly either on the north beach, the sand-dunes or north river wall. Ben agreed to look after Arthur's gun, and store it on top of the bake-house oven where the powder would keep dry. On occasions Arthur smuggled the gun home to clean it.

Arthur and Ben invested 10/- each in a gun-punt—a delapidated old thing that "Locker" Nudd had patched up—and called it "The Tub." They moored it on the North Quay and the local urchins had great fun towing her up river and rocking and floating in her.

"Mr. Patterson," said a woman one day to Arthur's father, "I saw your son on a boat going down the river early one morning." Had she told him she had seen a mad Brontosaurus in hot pursuit he could not have been more upset.

One of the channels, or "drains", on Breydon is named Ship Drain after the brig "Agnes" acquired by the Commissioners in the Seventies to sink in the mouth of the drain to act as a breakwater. All that was left to view of the old ship that had crawled regularly to the straits and back in the time of Nelson carrying cargoes of wine and fruit, were two rows of short, scraggy upright timbers. It was a favourite post of observation on Breydon.

One May morning Arthur and Ben tied up to the old "Agnes". Four avocets had been haunting Breydon for some time and Ben was eager to get a specimen, as were two noted wildfowlers—John "Pintail" Thomas and Jimmy Hurr.

The wildfowlers took a shot at the avocets from a distance of half-a-mile and missed. Meanwhile, Arthur took a shot and wounded one bird, and it fell slowly into the water and sat there, dazed. Ben took a shot at it over Arthur's shoulder—the shot almost broke his eardrum and gave him temporary deafness for days afterwards—they rowed over and snatched the victim out of the water, just as Thomas and Hurr punted up and banged into "The Tub" demanding the bird.

Ben pushed the trophy up under the forepeak. When the fowlers tried to claim it he threatened to lay into them, and would have done so if necessary. Arthur intervened at this juncture and suggested they compare cartridges.

"We use number 2's." said the fowlers.

"Very well," said Arthur, "we use number 5's. When the bird is skinned if any 2's are found in it, we'll come to terms."

They reluctantly agreed, muttering that they had done them out of a good day's work. When Ben skinned the bird, only 5's were found! Ben paid his partner 15/-for his share and maintained, all his life, that it was he who had shot it.

"Pintail" Thomas was one of the last of the professional punt-gunners. He and his wife kept a shop in Charlotte Street where they sold vegetables, meat and wildfowl. A Breydoner since birth, he went to sea as a cabin boy in a sailing smack and drifted back to the "flats" when he was strong enough to handle the smelt-nets. He inherited his father's old flint-lock gun and lost two or three fingers when

11 The wildfowler John "Pintail" Thomas

the heirloom burst.

His chum was also a good bird shot. Jimmy Hurr was a man of many parts—a stickler for open air sports, an authority on fowling pieces and a "wonder unto many." Born in Southwold, he became apprentice on a Sole Bay barge, later running away to join a brig and went to Hamburg. He left that and became a "fag" for the local cricketers at Cambridge and became known as "Jimmy Cricketer." He wedged into the Breydon fraternity but varied his occupation by repairing cricket bats and gear.

Arthur made no trouble of rising early. Having sat up late into the night bird-stuffing Ben Dye was slow to "come to," and on occasions he kept Arthur waiting two hours, then would dawdle and make him late for breakfast. On these rambles, Arthur was learning and noting much about the habits of birds and fishes. He avoided, as far as possible, in his nature notes, technicalities, confining himself to simple observations, and occasionally touching up with local colour all incidents and records. He wrote up nightly before he went to bed, and at any other time, if there was something to record.

Chapter VI

The Breadwinner

"What began unconsciously in the child, grew keener and stronger in his youth and in the more serious days of breadwinning." A. H. PATTERSON

A little girl scrambled to sit opposite Arthur at the double-sided desks when he was at the Day School. Her name was Alice Elizabeth Paston, and she was born in Yarmouth on December 12th, 1858. The two children kicked each other and passed notes under the desk, and at the age of ten, on School Treats, they became sweethearts.

Robert (Tom) Paston—Alice's father, a sawyer, was a young Wesleyan local preacher. He had courted Alice's mother at Primitive Meetings in the Hayloft, this "probably taking him there oftener than the spirit! Before they married, they cast lots—after making it a matter for prayer—as to which of the two should go over the the other's denomination. As is mostly the case, the Lady won—and Tom Paston became a Primitive preacher." Thus went the story Arthur told.

Arthur and Alice were married at the Primitive Methodist Temple, Yarmouth, on February 5th, 1880. The Reverend Frederick Broughton Paston, Alice's brother, who was a Primitive Methodist minister, officiated, and the registrar was Mr. Lovewell Blake. Arthur was 22, and Alice a year younger. Amongst the wedding gifts was a cloth hearthrug, a pair of shilling vases, a frying pan, a galvanised bucket and a set of stove brushes.

Their first home was a small cottage in Market Road, with two rooms up and two down with a backyard barely big enough to stand a water butt in. Arthur's birdstuffing, carpentry and tinkering about was done on the kitchen table, and the second bedroom served as a storeroom, where he kept a variety of pets. He recalled the story of his pet rat.

"Looks like large mesh wire netting?" Arthur suggested when Alice held up a spare blanket which revealed, when unfolded, great holes all over it.

"Wire netting," she gasped, "that's what your nasty rat has done for me!"

His pet white rat had bitten through several thicknesses of a folded blanket in order to make a nest. My great-grandmother was to have a great deal of discomfort in the years that lay ahead.

When he married Arthur's weekly wage as a relief postman was 16/-. On one occasion, when they got behind with the rent, he was able to pay off the debt by selling a few cases of stuffed birds at an auction. In between times, he peddled tea. Because of the insecurity of relief work he applied for a regular postman's job, but was turned down as "non-suited," because of his family's medical history, though was given an "auxiliary man's" job at 12/- a week. To supplement the wage, he worked as a ticket collector at the "Aquarium Theatre" for 5/- a week, working four hours a night—six days a week. This arrangement lasted three years. His

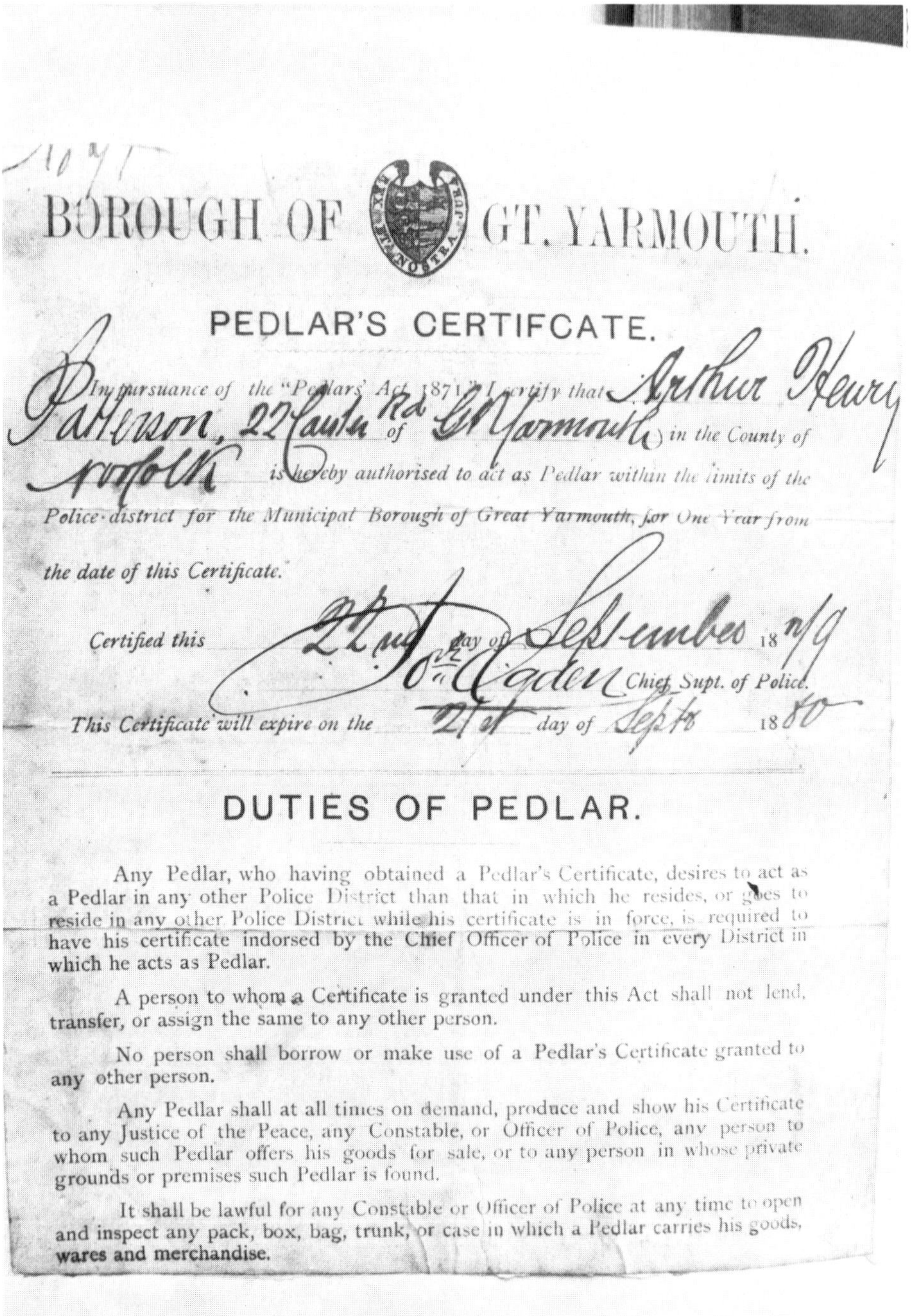

BOROUGH OF GT. YARMOUTH.

PEDLAR'S CERTIFCATE.

In pursuance of the "Pedlars' Act, 1871," I certify that Arthur Henry Patterson, 22 Caister Rd *of* Gt Yarmouth *in the County of* Norfolk *is hereby authorised to act as Pedlar within the limits of the Police district for the Municipal Borough of Great Yarmouth, for One Year from the date of this Certificate.*

Certified this 22nd *day of* September 18 79

Jno Ogden *Chief Supt. of Police.*

This Certificate will expire on the 21st *day of* Septr 18 80

DUTIES OF PEDLAR.

Any Pedlar, who having obtained a Pedlar's Certificate, desires to act as a Pedlar in any other Police District than that in which he resides, or goes to reside in any other Police District while his certificate is in force, is required to have his certificate indorsed by the Chief Officer of Police in every District in which he acts as Pedlar.

A person to whom a Certificate is granted under this Act shall not lend, transfer, or assign the same to any other person.

No person shall borrow or make use of a Pedlar's Certificate granted to any other person.

Any Pedlar shall at all times on demand, produce and show his Certificate to any Justice of the Peace, any Constable, or Officer of Police, any person to whom such Pedlar offers his goods for sale, or to any person in whose private grounds or premises such Pedlar is found.

It shall be lawful for any Constable or Officer of Police at any time to open and inspect any pack, box, bag, trunk, or case in which a Pedlar carries his goods, wares and merchandise.

13 Pedlar's licence taken out just before his marriage. He peddled tea

12 Arthur Patterson at the age of 21

afternoons were free for rambling and doing whatever he liked. They were trying days for Alice, who by then had three small children, but she never complained.

A newspaper article every now and again paid for his writing paper, and cases of birds bought the odd nature book after the rent had been paid. On winter afternoons he earned a little money at schools doing shadowgraphy. He constructed out of flat tin and zinc several sets of "puppets" one foot high. By the aid of not too tight rivets, the figures bowed, walked, and so on, the limbs being worked by wires, looped on the rivets. They did all sorts of things. The shows were given names such as "The Broken Bridge," "The Haunted House," and "The Menagerie." He cut out performing lions and elephants, trees, bridges and houses, and rigged up a gay frontage, with a linen screen, and a bright lamp behind. He "worked" schools and bazaars, charging admission at 1d. a time.

Later, in 1895, he wrote a book about the manufactured fun that could be made from shadows, called "Shadow Entertainments and How to Work Them being Something about Shadows and the Way to make them Profitable and Funny." In the preface, he wrote:

"Someone has said 'there is nothing new under the sun.' Whether that be true or not, shadowgraphy is no new thing, for in our grandfather's days, manufactured fun was from shadows . . . having myself 'worked' a shadowgraph somewhat above the average run of such exhibitions—making profit as well as fun, thereby, it has occurred to me to put the thing into 'black and white' for the benefit of those who may care to take advantage of my experience."

When Arthur and his family moved to a slightly larger house in Well Street, there was room in the backyard for a shed, which he turned into a menagerie. He acquired an armadillo, cockatiels, a noisy green parakeet, and some Abyssinian cavies. He made cages for the animals and engaged John Gillings, a carpenter who in summer exhibited a van of living creatures on Yarmouth Beach, to build him a tent, 9ft. × 12ft. On three consecutive Saturdays in April of 1883 Arthur set up his menagerie in the Market Place and hundreds flocked to see his main attraction—"The Crocodile Pig,"—Tommy, the armadillo. William Patterson would not go near the Market on those days. He considered his son was "going downhill fast!"

At Whitsun, having obtained leave from the Post Office, Arthur hired a Russian pony, bought a phaeton for £3 onto which he packed the tent, the cages of animals, and taking along two chums as assistants, they set out to put on shows in the Norfolk villages. Over 100 turned out at Acle to see The Showman and his Menagerie, and they travelled as far as Shipdam and East Dereham, stopping at villages along the way. Arthur slept in the tent, and his assistants occupied the phaeton. After the holiday, the profits were shared out and Arthur went back to the post.

"A typical day was spent as follows:

5.30 a.m.	(in summer occasionally 3 a.m.) Rise
6.00 a.m.	Letter sorting, until 1 to 1.30 p.m.
2.00 p.m. to 6 p.m.	Enjoying himself on Breydon, the beach, denes, or Bureside marshes
7 p.m. to 11 p.m.	Ticket collecting at the Aquarium Theatre"

At the end of 1883, Arthur, who was then 26, was offered a job as Keeper in Charge of a fine collection of monkeys, foreign birds and small mammals at Preston Zoo, by Francis Guy who was expecting to become Manager of the Preston Pleasure Gardens. The Gardens stood in a spot near the River Ribble where there was a dancing pavilion and stage, a football ground, a refreshment bar and the zoological gardens which latter was a favourite rendezvous of Preston people, who came in the hundreds on Sunday afternoons in tramcars. The Zoo has been mismanaged for some time, and having become very run down, Arthur's job was to try to get it back into some sort of order.

With the Post Office holding open his job for one month, Arthur and his family left for Lancashire. On arrival, they received a cool, almost insulting reception from the lodgekeeper-gardener and his wife, but he got on well with the chief shareholder. By careful dieting and sanitary methods, he reduced the loss of seven animals a week to an average of one death per month. Arthur made a feature of feeding the seals and monkeys, and in part of the wintergarden—a large, glass building in which grew trees—he introduced white herons, cockatoos, peafowl and doves, and called it "The Great White Aviary." He constructed other aviaries in the building, decorated the monkey cages with trapeze, and added to the Zoo collection Barbary apes, a flock of demoiselle cranes, a Mexican tiger-cat, Coali Mundi and a fox.

Arthur popularised the Zoo by submitting news paragraphs in local newspapers and distributing handbills, and wrote "A Descriptive Catalogue of the Zoological Department of the Preston Pleasure Gardens for the convenience of visitors" which sold by the hundreds at 1d. a copy.

Arthur took on an assistant—John "Menagerie Jack" Evers—a hard-working lad who paid his widowed mother's rent by breeding and selling guinea pigs and rabbits. John took over as keeper when Arthur left in 1884 until the Zoo closed down in 1885 and he obtained work in Manchester, later taking charge of the Great Monkey Show at Alexandra Palace in 1889. He went to Chile in 1911 and travelled with the "Boxing Kangaroo" to principal cities in Europe from Moscow to Paris.

Arthur had one day's holiday whilst at Preston and he and Alice spent it at Blackpool. On his afternoons off, they went to Liverpool. At the end of the year, they returned to Yarmouth, but a week or two before leaving the Zoo, whilst cutting up a horse's liver, the knife slipped and he cut his finger. He contracted blood poisoning which resulted in an outbreak of abscesses—36 in all breaking out in various limbs.

Arthur had no job to return to and they had little money. For three days he printed grocers' window tickets for Christmas display, when, fed up with idleness, walked into Palmers, the drapers, to see if they would give him a job.

14 With John "Menagerie Jack" Evers the lad he took on as assistant at Preston Zoo

Chapter VII

The Young Naturalist

"Naturework covered its own expenses. Six small children by now. If [wife] she grumbled she did not do openly . . . The happiest years of my life." A. H. PATTERSON

Arthur worked as a warehouseman at Palmers in Yarmouth Market Place for 5½ years. The warehouse in the Row was dark and gloomy but the spare hours he spent alone with Nature made up for it, and he enjoyed days out with his employer Mr. J. Hurry Palmer, who took him shooting at Martham and treated him more like an equal than an employee.

His first job of the day was to clean the mirrors in the gown and millinery rooms, and the glass chandeliers and globes, then unpack the deliveries and take them round to the various departments. He supervised the errand boys and packed up parcels for delivery. He was rough carpenter and general repairman.

He recorded a typical day in his diary:

"May 12th,	4.30 a.m.	Up and on Breydon. Saw spring migrants.
	7.30 a.m.	Home (on Denes) to breakfast.
	9.05 a.m.	At Work at warehouse.
	1.10 p.m.	Home to dinner. Pickled specimens in bottles.
	2.15 p.m.	At Work again. Sent 2 natterjacks to gentleman in London.
	8.10 p.m.	Home. Sent to Norwich pickled specimens.
	9.00 p.m.	Home again. Writing notes.
	10.00 p.m.	Off to bed."

Broken boxes from the warehouse were turned into cases for his stuffed birds, and the black surface paper from Irish handkerchief boxes proved excellent for papering the outsides. He salvaged white paper from woollens which he folded into quarto-size and had bound into notebooks for nature notes. On the wastepaper, he wrote the manuscript of his first book "Seaside Scribblings and How to make the most of a Holiday Jaunt," which was published in 1887. It contained a series of articles written for the "Yarmouth Gazette" in 1885 and 1886 on such local celebrities as the beachman, puntgunner, and bird-catcher, together with chapters "for visitors" which dealt with boating excursions, seaside fishing and other topics.

His second book "Notes on Pet Monkeys," the material for which he gathered from his experiences with monkeys at Preston Zoo, was also written on Palmers' wastepaper and was published in 1888. The following year, "Seaside Sketches", printed rather badly by a local firm, was a failure. When the author later saw some copies on an old book-stall priced 1d. each it helped him "keep humble." "The Amateur's Zoo" was published the same year; it was a book on "Pet animals, their habits, characteristics, and how to keep and treat them in captivity."

"Reeds—slender green reeds
Spear leaves and feathery fronds.
The best of all Nature's weeds
Livening broadsides and ditches and ronds."

Arthur wrote those words in his diary in 1889.

"9.30 p.m. Just been with my three oldest children for a saunter as far as the Bure walls—as much for a sight of a bunch of common reeds, [Phragmites communis (australis)] growing in a ditch close by the Tarworks. If there be anything in the vegetable kingdom that bewitches me it is the reed, when quietly reflecting itself in the unruffled pool or swaying and sighing before the blast of the roughening wind.

"If I ever get a fit of the 'blues' I always when convenient at any time of the day go and sit down by these reeds and regain my equilibrium."

As a child Arthur had found the seashore a source of wonder, for there was often some strange fish to be found washed up on the shore. The fishmongers' windows were a delight to the small boy, and his favourite job in his stepmother's shop was cleaning and gutting herrings and mackerel for her to "pot." As he grew older and went eel-catching and smelt-fishing on Breydon, he became interested in fresh-water fish.

In June 1881 he fell in with a beautiful fresh-netted example of the pinky-coloured Boar-fish (Capros caper) when passing the shop of a shrimpcatcher, and this brought him into contact with Mr. Southwell. (Thomas Southwell, F.Z.S., M.B.O.U., banker, and founder of the Norfolk and Norwich Naturalists' Society.)

Southwell had seen Arthur's short notes in the "Eastern Daily Press' and his first letter to him, which is pasted in his notebook, was full of cheery helpfulness. "I shall be at all times happy to assist you in identifying any bird, beast or fish, which you may feel doubt about, or any so rare or obscure that it may be desirable to have confirmatory evidence regarding it . . ."

From that time onward he sought a more intimate acquaintance with the fishes of his native county. He had a liking for prying out odd forms of marine life, so he engaged a disabled shrimper friend in an invalid chair to distribute to the shrimp boats paste-bottles half filled with formalin in which to pickle unusual finds. These were gathered in at intervals or shrimper boys called at Arthur's house with specimens for which he paid them 2d. for curios, and 3d. for rare fishes. He recorded the finds in the local paper.

"November 26th, 1889: This page ought to have been written in red ink, for tonight I was made a member of the Norfolk and Norwich Naturalists' Society—an unanimous vote running me in. I have to thank Mr. Southwell for this good and very unexpected (i.e. I never had hoped for such an honour) stroke of good fortune. I read a paper on Gulls and Terns: 25 minutes. Never felt in worse form; felt quite a *dwarf* amongst *giants*; small and insignificant. I wonder they tolerated me at all."

Thomas Southwell had proposed and paid his membership subscription and continued to pay it for several years, until Arthur was made an Honorary Member on April 26th, 1910. He went on to contribute to the "Transactions of the Norfolk

15 With James Beckett in 1887. The two naturalists shared an interest in microscopes. Beckett became a journalist for the "Eastern Daily Press"

and Norwich Naturalists' Society" for 40 years, describing and recording the birds and natural history of Yarmouth. His most valuable series was that on the fishes of Yarmouth and Norfolk.

Diary entry: March 11th, 1890.

"I never regretted more the lack of money—as an aid to Natural History research than now. What could I not do if I were a gentleman of means! If I'd only a few shillings more spare a week than I have now, I am confident I could double Day ("The Fishes of Great Britain and Ireland" by Francis Day, F.L.S., F.Z.S., published 1880-1884) only—the list of local fishes. Men will do a lot for 'tips' and if I could but afford—after putting the shrimpers on the hunt for small and peculiar fry—to pay them a little now and again for their trouble, I should be amply repaid. What one wants really to do is to induce the men to save *all* their refuse—all of them—and bring it for quiet rummage over—many a rarity and 'new' fish would be found."

"Spring 1890. The earth is the Lord's and the fulness thereof!—and no *naturalist* is the man who fails to see a Divine Hand in it all."

On June 15th he took a ramble with Ben Dye to Mautby by the river wall to the

16 Arthur Patterson at the age of 35

west end of Caister and round home again by road.

"The meadows," he wrote, "and marsh are smothered with the richest clover, grasses, the sorrel, intermingled, reddening with a glorious hue huge patches here and there, whilst the myriad buttercups in others yellowed vast tracts—these intermingled with white campions, marguerites [ox-eye daisies] and a host of others gave a varied aspect which was most delightful. The ditches are brimful of all kinds of vegetable life, the yellow iris, sedges, yellow water lilies and a hundred others catch the eye as the scarcely to be seen water veined the meadows in all directions. Cows fat and contented, with sleek holiday-making horses dotted the scene in all directions. Birdlife was abundant . . ."

Chapter VIII

The Showman

> "I was ever optimistic, like Mr. Micawber, but without waiting for something to come up I went out and did it."
> A. H. PATTERSON

Francis Guy, the man who had persuaded Arthur to take the job at Preston Zoo, was appointed Superintendent of Phoenix Park Zoo, Dublin in 1890 and in the September offered Arthur a job there as Head Keeper. Mr. Palmer urged him to go for a month's trial and Mr. Southwell said: "The new job might be the making of you." Alice and his family remained in Yarmouth.

On arrival at the Zoo, Arthur was installed, not as he had been led to believe, as Head Keeper, but as Handyman, Aquarium-minder and Cage-mender. After he had been there a week, Guy left him in charge of the Zoo, while he returned to England to pack up his home for shipment to Ireland. He owned a handsome, modern country house at Cornard Magna, near Sudbury, Suffolk, surrounded by tastily laid out grounds with lawns and walks, aviaries, small mammal houses, pens and runs—quite a miniature reflex of the big zoo in Regents Park.

Before Guy left, he gave instructions that Arthur should NOT write any natural history notes in the Press as all credit was to be due to him. Disillusioned, Arthur stayed long enough to save the money for the mailboat home. He arrived home with 2½d. in his pocket.

Next morning, he was down on the beach, happy as a sandpiper, drinking in the pure air; and the following day he gathered sufficient blackberries in the country for a reunion pie.

Diary entry:

> "My notebook has lost a month's entries, but I must slip in again and with renewed vigor make double speed in discoveries and in work accomplished."

With no employment to return to, Arthur filled his days with fishing, wandering and scribbling. He never spoke to his father, or anyone else, about his financial problems. In October he became a sewing machine agent for the Singer Manufacturing Company, a job he hated "like poison." He was not a mechanically-minded man, and at the end of the agency which lasted a little over a year, he had only sold 50 sewing machines and was still unable to understand how they worked. To supplement his income he dealt in livestock and books, and at Christmas acquired a booth in Yarmouth Market Place and exhibited "The Monster Elephant Fish"—his friend John Gillings' old stuffed sunfish (Orthagoriscus mola).

On April 14th, at the age of 33, he made his first contribution, an article on Rare Birds, to "The Zoologist," the important Journal of Natural History. In the same year "Fish-hook and Float" was published, a book about salt water fishing and

17 The Whale Exhibition at the foot of St. Peter Mancroft church in, he said, "the quaint-timbered old shanty at the corner of Norwich Market—next door to an orange stores—at the fish stall end"

fresh water angling round Yarmouth, written basically for the visiting angler. Arthur was grateful for £1.0.0d. which W. W. Spelman paid him for the manuscript "A List of Fishes of the Great Yarmouth District" with notes on each species, which Spelman intended to include in his book "Sojourn in East Anglia." When the list was published separately under the pseudonym "Luberta" in 1892, without Arthur's permission and with no acknowledgement to the author, he was deeply hurt. The list had taken him years to compile.

During 1892 Arthur was commissioned by the Secretary of the Norfolk and Norwich Naturalists' Society to write a book dealing with Broadland subjects. He called the book "Broadland Scribblings" and it was, he considered "the freshest and breeziest of my books." It was published under the pseudonym "Broadland Naturalist." The book contained sketches of birds, insects and fishes of Broadland and some of the well-known characters. The copyright yielded him £10.0.0d. which enabled him to meet his obligations during his remaining few weeks of unemployment.

He applied for a post as School Attendance Officer, but was turned down. The Chairman of the School Board is reported to have said: "I cannot see how a young man with his head full of beetles and things could settle to that sort of job."

An exciting incident occurred in Yarmouth harbour in June 1891. A seven ton, 30ft. Lesser Rorqual Whale (Baloenoptera rostrata) was bemused by the sandbanks off Yarmouth and found its way into the River Yare, where it was set upon by the Gorleston Lifeboat Crew. Armed with various weapons, it was harrassed, until, in one of its wild dashes at the quayhead, it smashed its beak [snout]. It was claimed by the Lifeboatmen, and hauled ashore to be exhibited in the Elizabeth Simpson Lifeboatshed where eager spectators viewed it at a penny a time. After a day or two, the beast became "high" and the body swelled up like a balloon.

An "Opening Ceremony" was arranged to which several town and country folk and a privileged public were invited to attend, and Mr. Shipley, veterinary, of Southtown was engaged to dissect and gut the whale. Arthur gave a lecture on the natural history of the Lesser Rorqual Whale, the beast was skinned and Walter Lowne, the taxidermist, was employed to stuff it for £30. It was hoisted onto a lorry and taken to his shop where some weeks were spent scraping the layer of blubber off, constructing a framework and a wooden "backbone" over which to stretch the skin, and stuffing it with straw. Over 1¾ cwt. of preservative were required to preserve the skin.

Walter Lowne had been apprenticed to the carpentry trade. He had lived next door to Arthur and both were interested in birds. Arthur lent him a book on taxidermy and Lowne went in for "bird stuffing" until he was confident enough to open up a business on Fullers Hill in Watson the Gamedealer's old shop. An ardent member of the local Angling Society, Lowne won many prizes at angling competitions, and became a leading, expert bird-stuffer and preserver of fish.

Messrs. Cockrill, Woods and Whiley, the lifeboat crew, formed a Show Company and arranged for the Whale to be transported to London. Arthur, who was out of regular work at the time, was employed as an attendant. He wrote a booklet about the whale and it proved a popular and profitable exhibition for the boatmen-owners. After the Whale's sojourn in London, it was transported back to Norwich.

Meanwhile, Cockrill hired a temporarily empty shop at the top of the Market Place at the foot of St. Peter Mancroft Church steps, in which to exhibit the Whale. Having failed to get a picture painted under £10.0.0d. he engaged Arthur to paint and have ready a huge oil sketch to decorate the front of the shop. He purchased sheeting 12 ft. square, stripped his front room wall of its pictures and rigged up a frame on which the calico was stretched. Arthur put his whole energy into the painting and made 40/- on the venture. Stephen Batchelder, the artist, aided him by some useful hints, and gave him a look every now and then.

Batchelder, a Lancashire man, took up photography when he settled in Yarmouth and in the Sixties and Seventies had a booth in Regent Road. His father painted panoramas and exhibited pictures at Yarmouth Fair, opposite Market Row, and Arthur had helped him with sound effects like thunder and the rattle of hail. Stephen inherited his father's love of painted canvas but went to art achool. Broadland was his favourite resort, Bure his favourite "pitch", and in the roomy boat, the "Smudge", lived among the reedy lagoons and alder-clad banks.

So in May 1892 Arthur became a Showman and took the Whale "on tour". "The city," he recorded in his diary, "is ablaze with 'Have you seen the Whale?' " He was at Norwich for two weeks, and met old friends and made several new ones. In June the "Wandering Whale" was hoisted onto a dray cart and at midnight they left Norwich to plod to Lowestoft—28 miles away. Folk turned out on the way to see them and exclaimed "Twor the biggest thing in the whald!" or "A Shark!" a "Summat" or else "Twor summat else!" They arrived in Lowestoft at noon, smothered in dust which the horses' hoofs had churned up in little clouds along the way.

For a week, Arthur attended the Whale at Lowestoft, in a canvas booth in the market place, then it was transported to Yarmouth where it delighted the visitors for the summer season in the old beachmen's shed on Marine Parade. He had handbills printed advertising it as "An Interesting, Edifying and Intellectual Sight. Every visitor to Yarmouth must see it."

At the end of September, he quitted connection with the Whale. He wrote:

"I . . . lived a whole summer season off a whale, and by the time I had finished with it, I was fed up enough!"

Chapter IX

"Old Arthur"

"Look out, here comes Old Arthur," two boys were overheard to say on the quay, "Hurry up, he can run like the Devil!"
A. H. PATTERSON

By the age of 35 Patterson had had a variety of jobs which included pupil teacher, Assurance agent, auxiliary postman, ticket collector, zookeeper, warehouseman, sewing machine agent and showman.

At the end of November 1892, the most troubled part of his life as far as getting a decent livelihood was concerned had come to an end and he began to earn a living wage. He was appointed School Attendance Officer, for a trial period of six months, subject to a month's notice on either side. His salary would be £60 per annum. The appointment was regarded as an experiment, as something had to be done about increasing school attendance.

It was said of him: "His attention will now be withdrawn from the exciting and interesting study of the tiny stickleback and the massive whale to the more tedious search after the *habitat* of juvenile specimens of the genus *homo*."

The new Truant Officer was authorised to patrol the entire town to seek out the offending boys—it is interesting there was no mention of girl truants—and railway trucks and the fishwharf were their favourite hiding places. Herring stealing was rife and truants from all over the town went to the fishwharf daily to steal herrings, which they sold to disreputable shopkeepers. Truanting was common with attendance at about 80%.

In those days before elementary education for all classes was as well established as it is now, the reluctance of the children to go to school was backed up by the apathy and hostility of parents. Confirmed truants were sent to the Southtown Truant School, where for a few pence weekly, they were given two square meals a day. It is no wonder parents encouraged them to abscond.

Armed with a long cane, which became his trade-mark, Old Arthur rounded up the boys from the fishwharf. They were given a thorough caning until they found difficulty in sitting down, and their parents were prosecuted. It was not uncommon to have seven summonses on a Saturday for non-attendance.

An amusing court case is accounted in the June 1902 edition of the "School Attendance Gazette," in which Patterson was featured.

"A boy's grandmother appeared, to give reason for his non-attendance. The old lady was very deaf, and all attempts to make her hear appeared fruitless, until Arthur Patterson appeared on the scene. Hastily taking in the situation, he procured a sheet of brown paper, out of which he improvised a trumpet and, putting the smallest end into the old lady's ear, he proceeded to investigate the case, the old girl declaring she 'could hear bootiful'."

In six months, through his efforts, a slight increase in school attendance was

HERRIN DRIFTER AT ORLEST

noted and there had been fewer summonses than in the previous year. The School Board, satisfied with his work, approved his reappointment as School Attendance Officer for the Yarmouth South District. In two years they were able to close the Truant School. This was about 1894.

His own son, John, played truant once, thinking he would get away with it. When he saw his father striding out along Southtown Road, he hid by the railway station, but he had been detected and was dragged off to school by the ear. He discovered *he* wasn't exempt from the cane either!

Patterson's methods of dealing with truants was original, and his hunting capabilities were compared with those of a bloodhound. His stepmother's disciplinary arrangements had taught him much which came in very useful when unruly boys had to be managed. One passionate boy lunged at him in a Row with a red-hot poker but he protected himself with his never failing cane.

The work kept him lively. He wanted to break the truants in and he had ways of curing them. In time he won their respect.

"The vast majority of children," he wrote in his autobiography "are naturally truthful, and it is abominable for anyone without cause to accuse a child of stealing or lying. A child's nature is peculiarly sensitive; and a wrong rankles long. As a boy, years' ago, I was watching mackerel being ferried ashore on Yarmouth beach in bullock boats [the strong, deep ferry boats that withstood the shock of being beached when heavily freighted] and, like most boys, thought a fresh fat mackerel a rare prize, if come by honestly.

" 'Master,' I said to the fisherman, 'give us a mackerel.' The man handed me one. I went home with it, delighted. My stepmother was a puritan in her ways and she accused me of stealing it. No protest of mine was accepted. She threw the fish in the street. To be branded a liar deeply cut me; I had rather been whipped. The memory of the mental picture of the episode remains vivid to this day. So I always start with a boy without questioning his honour, troublesome as he may be; I do not call him a sinner for truanting, but we both understand it is a breach of etiquette, a sort of bad slip that may lead to untoward incidents and reprisals."

Old Arthur was always willing to help young people interested in natural history. He told them stories because boys liked to know about birds, fishes and animals, and if he could get them interested in a tale, he had gone half-way towards winning their hearts. He possessed the gift of story-telling (in itself a sure road to the hearts of the young and the old) and his fund of knowledge must have been the envy of all members of the juvenile race who delight in the collection of beetles, caterpillars and birds' eggs.

In November 1912 a set of six cartoons was printed (100 copies for private circulation) as "A Souvenir commemorating 'My 20 years work as an Attendance Officer.' " By way of explanation, he wrote:

"This little souvenir marks the end of twenty years' Attendance Officership. My work has been congenial and has not lacked variety. When I commenced duties in 1892 the Town swarmed with truants and irregulars . . . I have endeavoured to do my best, and have, I hope, done my small share towards the betterment of our poorer children. In my experience there has been much pathos that touches, and not a little humour that tickles.

"In 1892, an Attendance Officer was often greeted by names not so inoffensive or dignified as his own, today he is a 'Mr' and is respectfully treated, while boys salute him with hands that are empty—if grimy."

18 Herring drifters in port in the heyday of the Yarmouth fishing industry

19 The School Attendance Officer 1899. At his desk in the Education Offices, 28 South Quay, Great Yarmouth. Note his cane

Chapter X

"Snubs"

"I laid aside my gun as an aid to natural history, having for a long time thought the poor little birds had quite as much right to live—and live happily—as I had."

A. H. PATTERSON

Whatever his occupation, great-grandfather found time to pursue his favourite hobby, and as a School Attendance Officer he had greater opportunities for rambles and observation. He was corresponding with Mrs. Eliza Phillips, founder of the Birds' Protection Society (formerly Fur, Fin and Feather Society) which was incorporated under Royal Charter in 1904, and renamed the Royal Society for the Protection of Birds and though he condemned "indiscriminate slaughter of birds," he saw "no harm in shooting certain species at certain seasons for food."

In April 1892 he started a newspaper agitation in favour of the Yarmouth Tolhouse being used as a museum. As early as 1262, it had been the seat of government and law, and had been in turn a collecting place for tolls, gaol, court of justice and assembly room. It was made useless when the Town Hall was erected in 1882 and prisoners were transferred to Norwich. At that time the only form of museum in the town was a dark, musty, underground room in the Tolhouse, used for storing stone carvings, old stones and the like which had been picked up from the débris of demolished houses. Patterson called it "The Lumbershop." He deplored the fact that "Bloaterville" (Yarmouth) has sent to Norwich the richest bird gems shot on Breydon and that he had presented many a rare fish to Norwich or the Natural History Museum, London, because there was no museum in his home town in which to house them.

A Museum Committee was set up with Mr. F. Danby Palmer as Chairman and Patterson was elected to the Committee. Norwich Museum offered the town surplus cases from the Lord Hastings' Collection subdivided at Melton Constable, and these formed the nucleus for the new local museum.

Meanwhile, during the 1892 Election, Patterson created fun and excitement when he displayed in the office window of the "Eastern Daily Press" cartoons on election matters. He was able to see the humorous side of any situation, so in May the following year began a weekly topical column in the "Yarmouth Mercury." It contained, he claimed, "a lot of harmless fun", and the series boosted the sales of the newspaper. Patterson desired to perpetuate the Norfolk Dialect, and "Melinda Twaddles Notions" as the series was called, was written in a language most of his humble townsmen could understand. The series ran until 1931.

I think an excerpt from Melinda Twaddles Notions written during the first world war might find a place here.

"Good Friday episodes:

"Well, frinds, I often think that if we know'd all what we eat, we wouldn't eat at all. My mother useter say to father, when she biled the taters not properly eyed—"Ah, bor, how'd yer row," she says,—"we all ha' got to eat a peck o' dirt afore we dye; and we mite as well do it furst as larst!"

"Don't tell me, maw," he'd say, "but let me hev things done properly." Yet he'd eat his fry'd sprats without removin scales, brains, harts and livers, and all that; and swaller whilks without takin the bones out, and sossidge with the skins on.

"I don't want no more of your saffern bungs!" (saffron buns) says Mrs. Pigwink to Mrs. Chittleburgh, "they pritty nigh kilt me." Then in cums Mrs. Ripshaw, and Mrs. Popcorn, and says the same thing.

"I'd like to know what you mean, you wimmen," says she; 'what's rong? You must hev bin eatin dry pidgen peas, or casterile beans."

"We hopes you aint bin usin arseynick!" gasps Mrs. Pigwink.

"No! my lady," says she, "I've bin using good bakin powder!" and she brings down 2 tins: one was marked BAKIN POWDER the other CARBINETTED SODER. She smells, and sniffs, and then she tastes, and turnin' white, sits down on a cheese box, what collapses, and drops her in it.

"Smellin solts!" she gasp, but we couldn't find it, so we shakes the pepper cruet under her nose, till she cums round.

"Oh deer!" she gasps, "if I didn't empty the powders in the rong tins!"

We all loox serious; but as none of us hed to git a horsepitel tikket, we presently busts out a-larfin.

No more of her bungs for me! . . . . . .

Yours as usurel,
MELINDA.

Birnt Lain Bungerlow,
Golleston.

In June 1893 Patterson and F. Danby Palmer called a meeting with a view to forming a local section of the Norfolk and Norwich Naturalists' Society (this was the third society to be established in Yarmouth). On June 15th, at the Friendly Society's Hall, Middlegate Street, the Yarmouth Branch was founded. Twenty-seven gentlemen gave in their names and Patterson was elected honorary secretary. Few members contributed to the Society, and it was difficult to keep a full programme once a month, so little by little numbers dwindled.

However, the Society had a stimulating effect on the Museum. Someone sent Mr. Carter, the Librarian, a bustard's egg that had been laid in a Coltishall aviary. It was in a box and somehow was forgotten for a few months. One day, Carter, insisted on blowing the egg. He handed it to Patterson, who assured Carter he could do better and handed back the box, standing back a little.

"Bang!" went the egg, "Whiz, bang!" The aroma was the worst Patterson has ever smelt. He fled, so did Carter, leaving Berry, the Tolhouse janitor to clear up the mess!

With the help of Corporation funds from the Technical Education Committee, a museum was built at the rear of the old Tolhouse in the block of Free Library buildings, approached from Middlegate Street. It consisted of two floors, but owing to light requirements, the upper floor was little more than a gallery. The walls were covered with a collection of paintings, and the natural history cases were placed underneath.

The Tolhouse Museum was opened with Mayoral and Corporation ceremonials in June 1895, and Patterson was invited to attend. He wrote in his diary:

"After being pretty well at the bottom of the movement, and having certainly been the means of securing, directly, the greater part of the exhibits in the Natural History Department—owing greatly to my being a member of the Norwich Society—not the slightest acknowledgement of my help and zeal in the movement was made. F. D. Palmer in his speech represented himself as the 'sole' and only projector and took to himself all the glory—to which he is welcome.

" . . . The Mayor's 'At Home' to which I was invited was anything but enjoyable to me, for I was here definitely snubbed by the flunkeys [servants] who neither offered me a cup of coffee or gave me one when I asked. After waiting half-an-hour—not all 'at home'—I slipped out and went up Breydon butt-picking—with Ben Dye, getting forty odd fish—here where I 'picked and picked' to the 'hank' of three or four herons and the wailing of some

20 Arthur Patterson on troll-cart outside the Tolhouse Museum. As he presented it to the Museum he insisted he should be photographed sitting on it

When he secured it in 1902 it was then the only one of its kind in existence and had been used by the firm of Lacon to convey casks of beer to Nelson's fleet. It was destroyed in the Tolhouse fire during enemy action in the Second World War and a replica may be seen in the present museum

curlew I WAS 'at home.' So endeth a day of snubs, . . . but what the deuce can an ordinary man without money expect at the hands of those with it and veneered over by the caste prejudices and petty selfishness of 'position and standing.' "

Arthur Patterson received recognition for "all the work he had done in reawakening in the town the study of Natural History which had almost lapsed since the days of Dawson Turner, the Pagets, and others," and "for his energetic and able efforts of the past 15 years," was presented with a microscope and Dr. Francis Day's "British Fishes." The occasion marked his resignation as Honorary Secretary in October 1898 when he was 41. T. J. Wigg succeeded him as secretary, and he and Patterson did their utmost "to keep the thing alive, but it petered out in 1905 for want of material to work upon."

The Tolhouse was gutted by fire in an enemy raid on Saturday May 10th, 1941. Only a small proportion of the exhibits was saved and much that threw an interesting light on the past was lost. The books of the reference library were also lost, though the lending library received comparatively little damage.

21 The Microscope presented to Arthur Patterson in October 1898 as a mark of recognition for 15 years natural history work in Yarmouth by members and friends of the Norfolk and Norwich Naturalists' Society

Chapter XI

The Naturalist

"I believe I am a naturalist now, for I can admire nature without the slightest desire to destroy. All God's creatures seem to me now just like little friends, with whom I hold sweet converse, and whose society I enjoy. I like to write of them as if they were personal friends; surely if they thought me now as harmless as I am they would not shun my approaches as they do my fellows." A. H. PATTERSON

"Of shooting birds," Patterson wrote much later, "I obtained a gun for shooting birds more to assist study than kill. I outlived the savage instinct to kill, but kept up my love for birds—all I can say in praise of a gun is that, but for it, and the feeling of power it gave me, I should never have gone out at three in the morning, or before daylight, in all sorts of weather, to get into birdland, year in and year out—after doing longer hours of hard labour the day before.

"Nowadays, a man or a boy can derive much joy from birdwatching without the desire to kill. But he who uses his eyes gets more fun out of a country walk than he who goes over the ground as if he were racing for a wager. A naturalist may do much with his eyes, but books are a tremendous help. They are the signposts which point a fellow to the correct road."

In 1893 the naturalist set about acquiring a boat as an aid to birdwatching and nature study. He wanted a boat to suit a naturalist—not a sportsman, a birdwatcher—not a butcher, so he commissioned a boatbuilder to build him a craft on the lines of the Breydon gun-punt. The Breydoners nicknamed it "The Fiddlecase."

The naturalist described the punt as 17 ft. long and 5 ft. abeam, and two-ended like a weaver's shuttle, an inch or so over a foot deep.

"Decked fore and aft with a low rail round the 'well', we care little for the wintry waves into which she dips her nose, for the broken water runs off at once from the slightly rounded deck . . . Flat bottomed and keel-less she floats in three to four inches of water, and 'over the flats' in shallows that a keeled boat dared not negotiate. The punt spelt speed and scant elbow room, squatness and easy management. One could bowl along with the tiller and sheet [50 square feet of tanned calico] in one hand and focus the field-glasses with the other."

He called the punt "Yarwhelp"—the local name for the Black-tailed Godwit (Limosa limosa).

Having secured a boat-shed in Cobholm in which to keep the "Yarwhelp", the naturalist set about acquiring a houseboat. He sold his menagerie and with the money purchased a fishing smack's boat for £3 and had an out-of-work friend put a low hut on top. He named the houseboat "Moorhen".

He had the houseboat taken up the River Bure to Mautby, where he moored it in the Mill Dyke on the opposite side of the river to Jim Banham's Marsh Farm. On May 18th, 1894, he recorded in his diary:

"Had the wife up a day, children too. It's rare fun providing for oneself."

On Whit Monday he took his first voyage up to the Broads, propelling the boat by a pair of oars worked from the cockpit smacksman fashion, and crawling at the rate of four miles-per-hour "like a huge snail." He moored at Acle and spent the week there. In the August holidays, he took "Moorhen" to Kendal Dyke and Hickling and "idled about" in the vicinity of Hickling Broad.

When Jim Banham moved to Lockgate Farm, two-and-a-half miles up Breydon on the north bank, Patterson took "Moorhen" there and moored her in the rond near the marshman's house. [The Banhams had been marshmen for generations and kept the banks and dykes in good repair.]

From the houseboat the naturalist was able to observe birdlife closely. All his studies had been taken up in a local and elementary kind of way. He recalled beginning the study of birds in 1877, the study of fishes in 1887, crustacea in 1889, with reptilia and mammalia all along. He enjoyed being alone with Nature.

"I dislike a hill," he said, "I love the level marshes and the lure of the muddy flats," and used every opportunity to escape to the houseboat, using the punt to get to and from it.

For those unfamiliar with Breydon Water, let us picture Breydon from the "Moorhen's" door. Banham's rond is roughly half way up Breydon, and the estuary is about one mile across at this point. When the tide is in we see what appears to be a great lake, with two parallel rows of posts or "stakes"—red on the one hand, tarred on the other, marking the main navigable channel.

But when the tide is out we see a different picture. There are mud-flats on either side of the channel and those in the north are intersected by narrow, deep runs or "drains"—with names like "North Wall Drain," "Five Stake Drain" and "Ship Drain." In nearby "Duffell's Drain" in an ideal spot for observation, is moored the Breydon Protection Committee's "Watcher's" houseboat.

To the right is "Stone Corner"—a little bay where the shore is entirely composed of tiny spire shells (Hydrobia sp.). The shells are several feet deep in places and at a distance the shore has the appearance of being a fine, sandy beach. In the distance, to the left, the outline of Yarmouth is visible.

We can see in Patterson's words:

". . . laden wherries, with huge gracefully swelling highpeaked sails, coming up on a fair wind, or tacking and quanting against a less favourable breeze. Here and there on summer days can be seen snow-white yacht-sails . . . and eel-catchers' punts. At other times, the blustering nor'westers flying down sombre shadows from cloudland, and the darkened surface of the water is churned into white crested waves; it is then wild and bleak by day, and the curtain of night falls upon a dreary and depressing scene. There are to be seen the most wonderful sunrises and the grandest sunsets.

"The outlook changes every hour. On fine days, even at low tide, when the flats are bare, amazing colourations—greens, browns, and golden—are seen at dawn and sunset; and at no season are they altogether unlively. And when the sun has set, and the stars themselves reflected in the cool depths; when the moon flings her radiance on rippling water and moist ooze; there is yet something to charm and enthral one."

"Breydon grows on one so," Patterson once said. He and Breydon were to become synonymous.

When the "Moorhen" grew leaky, Patterson had her drawn out of the water and elevated on Banham's rond near Lockgate Farm, and she provided him with both observatory and sleeping quarters. He obtained bread, eggs and cheese from the farm, and gathered mushrooms on the marshes to fry for his breakfast. He fished for flounders, eels and smelts. To warm himself be brought coal from home or picked up driftwood along the shore.

Jim Banham the marshman awakened him in the mornings by rapping his cowstick on the door; morning and night he patrolled his widespread domains to

22 Sailing "Yarwhelp" on Breydon in 1920

see if the cattle were safe and sound. "Mornin', Patt'son!" he would call, to which Patterson grunted a reply then snugged down for another hour.

He had good access to the rond by punt until the drain grew up, then only on the flood tide could he row the punt quite up to her, so he moored at Stone Corner and walked the 100 yards along the bank.

There on Banham's rond, the "Moorhen" ended her days

". . . her shadow cast over the sea scurvy-grass (Cochlearis officinalis) in springtime, the Michaelmas daisy (Aster tripolium) making a green round her in the autumn, while on summer days the scent of the wild southernwood (Artemisia maritima) that clothes the walls in big grey patches is not ungrateful. One can depend on the cabin, save in the winter months, being dry and habitable; in winter the now rather fragile skipper wisely sleeps at home!"

He sold the "Moorhen" to a gunner in 1914.

Another song of another Norfolker

Bor, I never cood arn much money,
  No matter how 'ard I try'd;
But never wor short o'dumplins,
  Or a good owd eel well fry'd,

Bor, I ha' found own Norfolk frindly,
  An' I married a Norfolk gal,
An' when I cum off o'the marshes,
  I've found her a good owd pal.

Law! I ha' lived wi' monkeys,
  And worked where the lions roar,
But I longed tu heer t' owd curlews
  "Whaup" front o' th'houseboat door.

So I drifted back tu owd Norfolk,
  And heer I intend tu 'bide;
For the bards, an' t' fishes, an' people
  Of Norfolk, air all my pride.

When Broadland is left for Jordan,
  And Charon cum over th' styx,
Du delve a deep hole in owd Norfolk
  Whose sile wi' my ashes shell mix.

John Knowlittle.

23 The "Observatory"—the old "Moorhen I" high and dry on a Breydon rond

24 Title page from a book of drawings prepared from Mrs Eliza Phillips, founder of the Royal Society for the Protection of Birds

Chapter XII

John Knowlittle

"I saw plainly, I should not know too much in the great field: I could hope to *know* but *little*, hence my coupling of the two words." A. H. PATTERSON

At the age of 39 Arthur Patterson adopted the pseudonym John Knowlittle.

"A naturalist," he wrote, "should be a specialist as a botanist, ornithologist, or entomologist. He may excel and in time be absolute master of his subject. I could see this but my mind is not a concentrative one, and I want change, variety and a vaster enjoyment. I prefer to dabble in every nature puddle, as far as my own East Coast corner is concerned. At his best a man can only grasp the fringes of any department of natural history in the course of a long laborious lifetime. Want of a scientific education, leisure, and not least—of means, were all against me."

As John Knowlittle, he attracted more readers to his articles in the local Press; and soon he became so well known and popular as a public speaker that he was, he wrote, "at every beck and call in town and miles out of it, so in self-defence I had hand-bills printed and made people pay for their fun."

His book "Man and Nature on the Broads" published in 1895 was dedicated to Mrs. Phillips, then Vice-President of the Society for the Protection of Birds, referring to her as "a devoted friend of the birds." "Rambles in Birdland," followed in 1896. The two books were reprinted from a series Patterson had written for the monthly Primitive Methodist Magazines "Springtime" and "The Aldersgate Magazine" and included sketches of the people and wildlife of the Broads. The stories appealed to children to be kind to birds and take example from their feathered friends. "Bird families," he maintained, "loved one another and human beings should do likewise."

In the same year Patterson wrote for the Society for the Protection of Birds a leaflet regarding the use of plumage in women's hats, entitled "Feminine Headgear, A Protest by a masculine naturalist." A member of the Society complimented him in saying: "It is writers such as you who do far more good than those not gifted with that charming style of expression. Girls will read yours when they will not look at a tract-like leaflet." The leaflet was widely distributed.

During the summer of 1897 John Knowlittle made a second trip on the Broads in his houseboat and his experiences "From the Log of the Moorhen" appeared in the "Eastern Daily Press." In the same year, he was invited by the Editor of the "Zoologist" to submit an annual report on Norfolk fishes. These and contributions to other aspects of wildlife were featured in the journal until it was brought to a finish in 1916.

"Life and Summertime," John Knowlittle wrote in his diary, "are all too short in this beautiful world of ours. The world is what we make it. Is life worth living?

'Life is good, for God did give it,
Good to all who rightly live it.'

A century would not be too long for a naturalist to enjoy it; it is a pity we do not have the opportunity."

In September he began a weekly series of local cartoons in the "Yarmouth Mercury" which continued until mid-1914, when they had to be suspended to make space for photographs of local men who joined the Forces. The first fifty cartoons were issued in book-form in 1898 with a sequel following in 1899. He contributed 975 cartoons in all on local topics to the "Yarmouth Mercury" as well as series in the "Evening News", "Eastern Daily Press" and other periodicals.

In November, 1897 he went as a special correspondent of the "Eastern Daily Press" to the scene of the Horsey Floods when the sea broke through. He called attention to the need of immediate action stating that "all the lowlands between the sea and the fine old city (Norwich) are in actual danger of being submerged." He exposed the Sea Breach Commissioners' apathy and neglect, and stated that he thought the River Commissioners, too, were "playing a dangerous game in so eagerly deepening the Yarmouth harbour mouth and otherwise experimenting at the entrance." Certain people considered him a "stupid alarmist" and in "Wildlife on a Norfolk Estuary" he predicted the sea would break through again at Horsey or thereabouts. (In 1938, 7,500 acres were flooded to depths which varied from a few inches to eight feet.)

John Knowlittle's next major book appeared in 1901. Reprinted from the "Zoologist" and limited to 100, principally for distribution amongst friends, "A Catalogue of the Birds of Great Yarmouth (giving a few descriptive notes when most of the rare species were obtained)" was the first complete list of birds of the district to be compiled since Sir James and Charles Paget's "Sketch of the Natural History of Great Yarmouth, 1834," nearly 60 years before. (They were the first to give us a word picture of Breydon and the hardy wildfowlers who frequented it.)

Amongst his artist friends was a Broadland artist who had gone unrecognised in his home town. Born in Yarmouth, he was, like Patterson, "A Child of the Rows." At the age of 61, Charles Harmony Harrison was hard up and had been seriously ill for several months. Patterson appealed through the local Press for Yarmouth to put on an Exhibition of his work, and within a month an exhibition was opened to the public, but whilst efforts were being made to promote it, Harrison died. However, he felt his efforts were rewarded "in time to push back the shadows that were beclouding the last days of poor Charles' life and let in a bit of sunshine." A touching tribute to the love of nature that made them kindred spirits was a bunch of bulrushes, fresh gathered rushes, reed tufts and faded reed-mace to lay on the coffin lid from one of his well-beloved Broads.

The Exhibition produced sufficient money to provide Harrision's widow with a small weekly allowance for several years. Patterson and Arthur H. Smith, a staunch watch-maker-philosopher friend, got together to write a memoir of "Charles Harrison, Broadland Artist". It was published in 1903 and profits from the sale of the work were added to the "Harrison Fund."

When invited to write a chapter about wildlife on Breydon for William A. Dutt's Book "A Guide to the Norfolk Broads," Patterson made the acquaintance of

Methuen and Company Limited, the publishers, and in 1904 they published his first serious full length nature book called "Notes of an East Coast Naturalist." It was illustrated by the Hunstanton artist he had befriended, Frank Southgate, R.B.A., who, before recognition, had added P.S.A. (Poor Stony Artist) to his name. The book contained a series of observations made at odd times during a period of 25 years in the neighbourhood of Great Yarmouth. The author intended it should "preserve much that future naturalists may not ever hope to meet with." The book was enthusiastically received all over the country as the work of a patient and accurate bird watcher and well received in the London Press. It secured for

25 Outside the Great Yarmouth Printing Company on Theatre Plain, Great Yarmouth. "My Share in the May Festival. I am dressed as Soldier Billy" wrote Arthur Patterson in 1898. He loved dressing up and in later years joined in the town carnival to raise money for "Hospital Day"

John Knowlittle a widely recognised position amongst naturalists.

On March 16th that year he was elected Associate Member of Marine Biological Association of the United Kingdom. He considered a great honour had been paid him by the Diploma.

Later that year, he recorded in his diary:

"1904. INCOME.

"Plodding away £90. 0. 0d. per annum. Hubbard, Income Tax bloke suggested I should pay Income Tax. I wish to Goodness I earned enough to conscientiously pay it! 13/14 books never brought in £15. 0. 0d. all told since 1884. My last—Hayloft to Temple manuscript I actually gave to Primitive Methodist Connexion and they said they lost by it. Methuen is first to offer ROYALTY on anything I ever wrote and I don't get a penny till

26 One of a thousand cartoons contributed to "The Yarmouth Mercury." It depicted suggestions for the May Festival

next Christmas. Cartooning is done with no security—no written agreement. I OUGHT to be earning enough to pay TAX, but Providence does not yet see fit!''

27 Charles Harmony Harrison, Broadland Artist

28 Portrait about 1906

Chapter XIII

Lord Mudflat

"The Dear Duchess" ALICE PATTERSON

Amongst the fellow-naturalists with whom Patterson corresponded was a Duchess, Mary of Bedford, an eminent ornithologist. She wrote to the naturalist in 1903 asking his advice on birdwatching in Broadland and placed an order for two of his

29 Caricature from sketchbook presented to the Duchess of Bedford in 1906

books, "Man and Nature on the Broads" and "Charles Harrison, Broadland Artist."

Pasted in his diary, is a letter, dated September 26th which reads as follows:

"I beg to acknowledge the two books which you have sent me and also to thank you for the little sketch which I am very pleased to have. I was very welcome to come to a 'houseboat' when walking from Berney Arms as it afforded me from the cold whilst eating my frugal luncheon. Perhaps it was yours? If you will write again at any time I should be glad to know what you consider the best time for visiting the Broads to see the waders. I envy you your talent for drawing what you see in nature."

Mary DuCaurroy Tribe, daughter of a Hampshire minister who became

30 "The most delightful remembrance of all!" Chatting to his "noble, lady friend" in the library at Woburn Abbey

Archdeacon of Lahore, became Duchess of Bedford when her husband Herbrand assumed the title after his brother, the 10th Duke, died. A lady of a multitude of interests — nursing, aviation, ornithology, ice-skating, fishing, photography, painting and handicrafts, she was a first class shot and excelled at everything she did. She designed and built a hospital in the grounds of Woburn, and became a qualified theatre sister and radiographer.

In March 1906, Patterson was invited by the Duchess of Bedford to Woburn Abbey. In his diary, he wrote:

"RED LETTER DAYS: I visited Woburn on March 9th, spending the night at the residence of Miss Brown, her Grace's secretary — who, with her Mother, are charming

31 The Duchess arrives unexpectedly

women. The carriage met me on the Saturday morning at 10 and 'Lord Mudflat' [he gave himself the nickname] drove in style to the Abbey where a warm-hearted and queenly welcome awaited me. After a chat in the Library (Good Heavens! the Bird books!) Her Grace drove me a four-hour canter round the magnificent grounds where I made acquaintance with Père David's Deer, the Saiga Antelopes, Aurochs, Zebras, Kangaroo and a host of other deer and Ruminants, all enjoying themselves in a semi-wild condition. [The Duchess of Bedford was awarded the Geoffroy-Saint-Hillaire medal "in recognition of her successful acclimatisation of deer and antelope at Woburn Abbey" — the highest award at the disposal of the Société Nationale d'Acclimatation de France.] Spent the evening in most agreeable conversation with her."

He continued: "Saturday morning found me wandering on my own. Drove up to the Abbey after dinner and had another enjoyable conversation with the Duchess whose knowledge and keenness for nature only equals her kindness. Much that I saw and conversed on is too sacred to jot down here and must live in my memory — as nice to ruminate on, and a joy to recall . . . Her Grace won my heart by her charming and unaffected good nature, even more than by her generosity . . . Sunday night came all too soon, and the thrill that passed through one when her Grace warm-heartedly bade me *adieu* is one of the holy remembrances of my life. No-one could mix with such a Queen among women, and visit Woburn, without being elevated, and stirred, and educated. *Vive! Mary of Bedford*!"

32 Bookplate commissioned by Her Grace the Duchess of Bedford in 1906. Arthur Patterson designed several bookplates for friends

Whilst at Woburn the Duchess told him she had put forward his name for Associateship of the Linnean Society of London and promised to back him up if ever the chance came along. The Society, founded in 1788 by Sir James E. Smith at Burlington House, Piccadilly, was restricted to only 25 associates.

"I had, for a long time," Patterson wrote, "in my inmost heart, desired to honestly and deservedly win the distinction of A.L.S. never once thinking myself really worthy of it, or ever anticipating such a reward."

Soon after his return home, a great crate of heads and horns arrived in Yarmouth. He had asked the Duchess if he might take a stuffed animal home with him or a pair of mounted horns to place in the Tolhouse Museum. In the crate were:

"1. Atai's head, antlers beautifully branched and in perfect condition.
2. Head of Caucasus red deer with equally fine antlers.
3. Sing sing antelope head, with long pointed horns beautifully twisted at base.
4. Three sets of antlers mounted on shields."

He was proud to place the fine and costly collection in the Picture Gallery in the

33 Pieces from the Royal Worcester teaset handpainted by George Johnson presented to Arthur Patterson in 1908 by Her Grace, the Duchess of Bedford. Each piece shows a different view of a moorhen, the bird which gave the name to his three houseboats

Museum.

The Duchess of Bedford commisioned him to produce a bookplate. She said: "The bookplate must be on my terms or not at all. If I pay for it — I can tell you if there is anything I don't like about it, and if you do it on your terms I cannot and will *not* . . ."

She visited Norfolk later that year and after spending a day alone on Breydon she motored to his home in Southtown. Patterson took her out on Breydon in the punt and they visited Jary the Breydon Watcher and the "Moorhen."

The Duchess admired the naturalist and sent him many gifts, amongst them a barometer, binoculars, a tiepin, and a teaset. She sent him grouse and salmon from her shooting and fishing expeditions in Scotland on many occasions and a turkey at Christmas.

On his visits to London great-grandfather lunched with the Duchess at her residence in Belgrave Square. His young son Gerald or my grandmother usually accompanied him and they stayed with Miss Brown from where they visited the Natural History Museum in Cromwell Road and the Zoological Gardens in Regents Park. The Duchess corresponded with great-grandfather until his death. She sent him accounts of her birdwatching expeditions and her letters are pasted in his notebooks.

The Duchess was an aviator, clocking up 200 hours of solo flying, and became known as "The Flying Duchess."

I found a postcard from the Duchess dated 1932 on which she wrote: "I flew over you today at 12.50 p.m. Did you feel anything in the air? If you see a little emerald moth in the air with lettering G-AAAO some day you will know who is inside."

In 1937 "The Flying Duchess" did not return from a solo flight over the Wash in her de-Haviland "Gipsy." Four struts from the plane were washed up along the east coast. The verdict of her death remained an open one.

Chapter XIV

The Family Man

"After dark, dawn." A. H. PATTERSON

Although his diaries have been invaluable in the research of my great grand-father's life, they were essentially nature notebooks and rarely did he write about his family.

His work of "kid-hunting" as he called it kept him busy and in spite of all his nature work, never failed his duties.

He wrote: "I am sure there are very few who write who sit down at night as I do exhausted in body and worried by a day's hard visiting. I often make as many as ninety calls on erring parents in a day. Last night I sat down fagged and with a blistered foot and underlinen damp with the perspiration of the day. I have frequently sat down to scribble and had to desist after a few lines and tumble into my bed, my brains absolutely refusing to assist my fingers."

At the end of 1904, on conclusion of his manuscript "Fauna of Yarmouth," great-grandfather was taken very ill. After a bad attack of influenza he suffered severe nervous exhaustion which incapacitated him for three months. It was an anxious time for his family and fellow townsmen. He had many visitors call at the house, from the mayor with a cheery word to a poor Breydoner with half-a-dozen eggs. The rest revived him.

By the beginning of February, he was "on the mend" and able to take a short walk on March 1st leaning on great-grandmother's arm. Some of the Norwich naturalists clubbed together and sent him to recuperate, at their expense, in the country and with the money left over he bought new Zeiss binoculars. He visited renowned bird haunts at Wells, Reedham and Scoulton Mere, but did little on Breydon being, he said "susceptible to fatigue."

When "Nature in Eastern Norfolk" was published in 1905 (Methuen the publishers changed the original name "Fauna of Yarmouth") Patterson included in it an autobiographical sketch, which he thought might prove helpful to young and aspiring naturalists who were experiencing difficulties which he himself had overcome. His next book was published the following year and was called "Wildlife on a Norfolk Estuary."

New Years Day 1908 found the Pattersons living in "A new domicile — 32 Lichfield Road, Southtown. A nice job," he recorded, "removing — of worry, labour, expense." At the end of January he invited friends Arthur Smith and Ben Dye and seven or eight others to a "Swan Supper" at the new Ibis House. Because of his love of the Breydon men and their customs he had revived the old time supper the gunners had enjoyed. In his diary, is recorded: "Tasted the gastronomic qualities of a 23lb. second year swan which I found tender and well-flavoured."

During his holiday from school-work in the summer of 1909 he visited several places in Suffolk for the purpose of gathering information for his "Rough Notes on the Fish and Fisheries of East Suffolk." From his diary, it appears he liked Aldeburgh most of all where, he said, "I enjoyed myself helping and talking to the fishermen. I would choose that restful seaside town if I ever wanted to be idle and absolutely quiet." The "Rough Notes" were reprinted from the "Zoologist" for private circulation in February 1910.

A second Swan Supper was held on March 7th, 1912, when twelve veteran punt-gunners and Breydon men, and one or two ardent naturalists met around the supper table of John Knowlittle. The festivities were reported in the local newspaper.

34 Ibis House, 32 Lichfield Road, Great Yarmouth, The room with the bay window on the corner was the naturalist's study or "den." Former homes at 50 Olive Road and 273 Southtown Road were also named "Ibis House"

Bob Vincent (father of Jim, the famous "warden" of Norfolk's bitterns and harriers) the Hickling eel-man, arranged for a 21lb. 12oz young mute swan shot by a local gunner to be sent to Yarmouth market on the Saturday and which "J.K. bore home on his shoulder from the marketplace . . . Mrs Knowlittle and two Knowlesses [my grandmother and her sister-in-law Florrie] spent a considerable time plucking the bird and preparing it for the following night's feast. The bird was cooked by Ben Dye, the baker who provided a long tin in which it was covered over with some dough 3 inches thick, and gave it several hours baking by which time the crust (not intended for consumption) was reduced almost to a cinder, but the swan with its ample stuffing lay lush and brown beneath.

35 The naturalist sitting outside the gate of Ibis House in 1912

36 "John Knowlittle carried home on his shoulder from the Market Place a young mute swan shot by a Hickling gunner. It weighed 21 lb. 12 oz."
It was for the second Swan Supper held in 1912

"It was borne by Dye to Ibis House. Mr Strike, the restaurant proprietor of Church Plain acted as carver-in-chief and gave generous helpings of breast, leg or wing, the 'parson's nose' going to the host. John assisted in loading the plates with cuts from a sirloin of beef (the customary practice) and luscious onion sauces, potatoes and greens. Plum pudding and custard followed, which was washed down with coffee and mineral waters."

When the cloth was removed, the 'churchwardens' (long-stemmed pipes) were filled and the yarns began. There followed interchange of experiences, Breydon stories and up-river escapades, and bird-lore and bird-life were discussed. Ben Dye gave a recitation and sang "Jolly Old Boys" with "Fiddler" Wigg on the violin. J.K. did the "Orange Dance" then handed round "the orange fruit", and read a chapter from his forthcoming book — the theme of which was "the consumption of a twin rabbit pie!" Mrs Knowlittle gave a well-delivered recitation and at 11.30 the Supper drew to a close. "He's a jolly good fellow" was sung in recognition of J.K.'s hospitality, with "Three Cheers" for the ladies who had prepared and served up the feast so handsomely.

During the summer Patterson took his youngest son to Regent's Park Zoo to interview the Superintendent and Head Birdman, with a view to Gerald becoming a keeper. They spent a grand day at the Zoo and Gerald was engaged as Keeper in Charge of the Insect House. He had proved to be the only child really interested in natural history.

In November, on a less happy occasion, Patterson went to London to take Alice to hospital. The Duchess of Bedford, his "noble lady friend" had made arrangements for Alice to see a specialist at King's College Hospital. Several years before, she had fallen at home through a trapdoor which one of the children had left open, and damaged her wind-pipe.

On his return to Yarmouth, Patterson wrote in his diary: "A lonely house is far more lonesome than loneliest Breydon."

Alice returned home just before Christmas after a month in London, and a serious operation to the throat and vocal cords, the latter having been removed.

Diary entry: January 1st, 1913. "The best item of natural history on this date is the continued progress towards recovery of my beloved wife."

Chapter XV

The War Years

"Let your motto be — Always at it — living to be of use in the world — and to 'interest others.' That's good enough for a naturalist, isn't it?" A. H. PATTERSON

In his diary Frederick Cook remembered his first acquaintance with Arthur Patterson and the above advice he gave him.

"My friendship with A.P. began in September 1909. I was a lad of 17. My father knew him as a local Primitive Methodist preacher. He and I cycled over to Yarmouth one Saturday morning and met A.P. at his home at 50 Olive Road (he was then 52). I can still remember his room, packed with books and papers and the paraphernalia of a naturalist's hobby. Thus began a close friendship which lasted 26 years and became a great influence on my life."

Frederick Charles Cook, a tailor by profession, but who swapped it for work as a local government officer, was a "bird-man." However, being a Lowestoft lad where fishing played an important role in the town's industry, he too was interested in fish. Patterson encouraged Fred to note down everything curious or interesting seen during the herring fishing — "large, very large fish, curious fish, queer circumferences, etc." then to take his notes to him when he was compiling his "Annual Notes" for the "Zoologist." He urged Fred to write to the Press about fish rarities and birds he had observed in the Lowestoft area.

Fred's notes proved to be reliable and interesting. He was a diligent watcher and recorder of the migration of small birds in the neighbourhood of Lowestoft, and, in 1913, his first article under his own name appeared in the "Zoologist." Fred soon made a name for himself in the field of natural history. He was a founder member of Lowestoft Field Naturalists' Club, being chairman for 7 years, and made an Honorary Member in January 1968.

Great-grandfather was in his mid-fifties when War was declared in 1914, and his five sons volunteered for active service. He continued to study nature as far as he was able and wrote in his diary on April 11th, 1916:

"So far, even amidst 'war alarms' I have kept going and at the age of fifty-eight am still eager to add new incidents to my notebooks and to put into print for the interest of others so much of what has (and still does) interest me. I seem to have crowded a lot of many things into my life, work, worry, anxiety, ink, pencil, and rare enjoyment. And I sincerely hope that a portion of mankind has not been the worse for my life and labours.

"Raids, Zeps, and the Dickens know what! Five bombs fell in the mud the other night on Breydon making holes big enough for the houseboat to float in, " he wrote in a letter to Fred Cook. [He had, in fact, had a lucky escape. Banham, the marshman, told him a Zeppelin passed over the "Moorhen" just after he left and to lighten herself dropped the bombs. A fight took place with an aeroplane and the Zeppelin fell into the sea early the next morning.] My Jack is musketry instructor at Sittingbourne, Gerald and Gilbert in France.

Other two boys [Arthur and William] also in khaki. Everyman, except shrimpers, seem in khaki. Hope fate will treat you well. Give my love to wife and accept my best wishes, old man, and let's hope the War'll soon be over, so we can go a-winklin' again."

Early in 1917 Patterson was informed that Gerald, his naturalist boy, who had been missing since October 1916, had been killed at The Somme, France. His heart was broken. To keep his mind off his grief, he scribbled "The Snipe-shooters Club" which was, he wrote, "the funniest book I have ever been on." Frank Southgate, his artist friend, like Gerald, died "hearty and reckless" in France.

During the War, he heard that copies of the "Yarmouth Mercury" containing "Melinda Twaddles Notions" went round the boys until they were too dirty and dog-eared to read. Patterson was pleased that Melinda had borne comfort to the boys amidst the squalor and degradation of the trenches, and brought them a little closer to old Yarmouth.

In January 1918 a fragment of German bombshell slightly damaged Ibis House. Not wishing to see his life's work destroyed, he made the decision to place at Norwich Public Library for safe keeping, his manuscript notebooks from 1878 to 1916, including original articles and letters; a complete set of his political, football and fishing cartoons; drawings; and a set of his published books. In a letter to the Public Library Committee he said:

37 Envelope sent to Fred Cook during the 1914-18 War

"Having received an intimation from the Germans — in the shape of a fancy brick smashed by them last Monday, 10 inches below by bedroom window — besides other unkind visits from them when on the water — I have considered it only right that my life's work should not be bust up, whatever they may or may not do to me."

Whilst he felt they would be appreciated at Great Yarmouth, he decided to give them to Norwich, because, at that time, the City was not vulnerable to gunfire.

"Norwich," he said, "was the intellectual centre of Norfolk, and my father and grandfather were Norwich citizens," and he wished them to be "preserved for the use of students in due time."

George A. Stephen, F.L.A., Norwich City Librarian wrote a "Readers' Guide" to Arthur Patterson's Life and Writings in July of that year on which I have based the bibliography for this book.

38 With youngest son Gerald Phillips just before his death on the Somme, France

Chapter XVI

The Lay Preacher

"No man liveth unto himself." ROTARIAN MOTTO

Patterson's parents had hoped their son would one day become a Methodist minister, and he was persuaded to take up lay preaching. He made his first attempt at Ormesby St. Margaret, where he went, one Sunday, clutching a much sweated

39 A group of lay preachers at the back of Queens Road Methodist Chapel. Arthur Patterson is standing on the right in the back row

over address, ready to "do battle." The gaping crowd before him was too much, and he dried up!

The next attempt was made at Martham. Fred Reed, an old hand at the job, had told him to treat the congregation as if they were a "patch of cabbages." It was July. The day was hot, and the atmosphere in Chapel drowsy. Whilst Reed (whose ambition was to become a full-blown parson) led the congregation in prayer, the young lay preacher got into such a flummox that, while heads were bowed in silent devotion, he collected his hat, and tiptoed out. Poor Fred's face must have been a picture when he rose and turned to give out the next hymn.

However, Patterson gained confidence and became a very well received amateur parson and usually found "a goodly crowd at chapel." (He recorded once he preached for the Primitives 1,788 times). The officials and authority urged him to study for the regular ministry, but he had high ideals of what a parson should be.

"The non-conformist bodies of that time," he wrote, "had committees made up of retired pork-butchers, drapers, coal-dealers, the ignorant and illiterate, and the parson had to be pachydermatous [thick-skinned] as he was continuously being subjected to analysis, criticism and scandal. I would always have been in hot water!"

There is on the River Yare four miles from Yarmouth just beyond Breydon, a hamlet called Berney Arms. It took its name from the inn, which, with the mill a

40 "Off to an appointment"—a drawing from his book about Primitive Methodism in Yarmouth "From Hayloft to Temple"

few yards upstream, has lately developed into a popular tourist stop for river traffic. The mill has been restored and is in the care of the Department of Environment, is open to the public and is a landmark for miles in every direction. The seventy foot high red brick mill was built originally for grinding clinker for the Burgh Castle cement works across the river. When the Cement Works closed down the mill was utilised for draining purposes and it stopped working in 1949.

Sunday after Sunday John Bitton the regular Sunday preacher at Berney Arms preached the Word at the hamlet saying: "Now then, the souls at Berney Arms want saving as well as many others." This earned him the nickname "The Bishop of Berney Arms." Sometimes he took along a lay preacher for company.

One Autumn Sunday Arthur Patterson and George Mayman, a twine-spinner by trade and popular lay preacher, accompanied the "Bishop" to Berney. They tramped across the marshes to the foot of Burgh Castle walls and, as was the custom, signalled the workmen's boat to be rowed across to pick them up. A gale was blowing, and after much signalling, the boatman reluctantly crossed over. Arthur told George to sit in the bows of the old smack's boat, which he did "silly-like" being not much of a waterman, and his companions sat aft. When the boat ducked in the huge waves, George made an excellent screen for them, and in so doing got drenched to the skin with salt water.

41 The President and members of the Mutual Improvement Society, 1878. Arthur Patterson is seated on the front row third from the left

A congregation of two was drummed up from the cottages on the lonely marshes and George Mayman appeared in the "pulpit" in the brushed-up brick-floored parlour lent them by the landlord of the inn, dressed in marshman's trousers which came nearly up to his chin, and would almost have made a suit for him! The collection amounted to 1½d.

Afterwards, the gale having increased, the "Bishop" decided to stay the night, so Arthur and his companion crept home along the Breydon "walls," almost blinded as the salt spray broke over them. Tired, hungry, drenched and chilled, the young lay preacher was greeted with nothing but abuse from his stepmother for arriving home so late and in such a condition. Patterson wrote later in life:

"Probably that night's discord lost me a white choker and a parson's bobtail coat . . . For some time I left the company of the sheep for that of the goats."

In late 1875, Patterson who was 18 and other lay preachers felt the need of "self-improvement" and formed a society for this purpose. Of it, he wrote: ". . . our studies at first were mostly reading and criticism of the Bible. Then we launched out into original effort, myself starting with a short paper on 'Punctuality.' " In December 1876, they formed the Mutual Improvement Society, set up for training young men for debate and pulpit work.

In 1890 the lay preacher introduced a new feature in the shape of "Lightning Sketches" as an aid to teaching the Infants' Department which had been separated

42 A blackboard lesson from "From Hayloft to Temple"

from the older scholars in the Sunday School. The method, he found, impressed on the minds of the little ones gospel and moral truths. One of his best known stories is told by Jack Hacon who remembered Patterson visiting his school in Church Road, Gorleston.

"Mr. Patterson," he recalled, "sketched on the blackboard a lion and a missionary. With a lightning flourish of the duster, he wiped off the missionary, enlarged the lion's stomach, and asked 'Now, where is the missionary?' Of course, we all shouted 'Inside the lion!' " He continued to teach in the Sunday School for many years and visited schools to talk to the children. His gift of story-telling made him always a welcome visitor.

43 A typical pen-and-ink sketch of spoonbills on Breydon

Chapter XVII

The Speaker

"I am being drawn into all sorts of places to talk (they will persist in the word lecture which I detest) . . ."
A. H. PATTERSON

Arthur Patterson was a popular speaker at village societies, literary societies, women's guilds, and all sorts of places and institutions. He illustrated his talks in a number of ways.

Sometimes he used a blackboard on which he drew lightning sketches, but more popular than that were the lightning sketches thrown on the floor and which the audience scrambled to procure for a souvenir. These were on double crown paper and executed in coloured chalks, crayons or charcoal. He also used oil paints in tubes and a fine and a broad brush that he dipped in clear turps and dashed onto the paper — the colours fixed immediately, although he said "the smell remained for hours."

In November 1926 at a meeting of the British Legion in the Holt Drill Hall, he gave a two-and-a-half hour talk on "Birdlife of the Broads." Twenty rough and gaudy lightning sketches in pastels helped to raise £12. 7. 0d. for the organisation. He recorded in his diary: "I am glad to have helped here."

He drew from an enormous repertoire of subjects and was able to illustrate subjects like "The fish-eating birds of Norfolk and Suffolk," "Some interesting Folk I have known," "Some little Nature Chums," and "Boyhood Memories."

He was a self-taught artist, having, apart from Wallis' teaching at the Day School, had only one lesson in drawing — from Frank Southgate, which gave a few hints on perspective.

He gained for himself a reputation as a local cartoonist, having made a study of "physogs" (facial expressions) and used them in his cartoons. Often his sketches included a self-caricature. He wrote at great speed with quill or fountain pen and sketched in an easy, flowing style.

Great-grandfather enjoyed a joke — in spite of his seriousness — and liked to play pranks on people, though he did not like to see friends made to look fools. When some highly respectable Norfolk naturalists testified to having seen a luminous barn owl, he refused to accept that this was anything but the result of a hoax. He quarrelled violently with several learned members of the county's Naturalists' Society over this both in private correspondence and the press, and even threatened to resign from the Society as a result of it.

"July 7th, 1920" diary entry: "Rather a knock out for him! I gave a lecture at the Technical Institute, Norwich, to the members of the Photographic Convention last night —July 6th — 'On the Broads.' Owing to the members getting wet on their excursion to Castle Acre, the meeting began at 8.30 instead of 8. At 8.20 I was standing near the platform doorway when an old gentleman courteously offered me a seat in the front.

'You are perfectly welcome,' said he, 'take a seat.'

'Thanks,' said I, 'but if I don't care for it, can I go up there?'' pointing to the platform chair.

'Oh, no sir. That's reserved for the lecturer!'

'Very well,' said I, 'if I don't feel comfortable here, I shall take the liberty of GOING on the platform,' which seemed a trifle to fluster him: I'd like to know what he thought of me when I was asked up by the Chairman . . .''

At another meeting he related a story of an experience as a taxidermist.

''A man came to me in tears with a dead cat,'' he said. ''He was willing almost to give me the church steeple if I'd stuff his poor dear. I said no, but he was a man who would not take no, so I yielded. By the time it was stuffed and dry he had forgotten about it. Not being a taxidermist, I did not take a deposit. When I took it home, he swore it was not his cat. I said it was. He said they were not the same eyes. I admitted they were glass. He said the expression was not the same as his cat's. No more would yours be if you had been stuffed for months! And with that he shut the door.

''I'd got a bit sick of the wretch, so when bringing it homewards, I stood it in the dusk on a doorstep and watched events. Up came a dear old girl, and stopping to pat it, over it rolled. The poor old lady was horrified and probably thinking it epileptic, precipitately bolted. I still watched, then up came two boys, and finding a good subject, started playing football with it.''

Great-grandfather was a popular speaker in schools and wrote articles in words which appealed to children. The following is an extract from a letter pasted in his diary from the Headmistress of Crook Place Girls' School, Norwich, which he took as a compliment.

''11.10.26. Dear Mr. Patterson.

You will be interested, I think in the following incident and will enjoy a child's compliment. After discussion last week on the life of St. Francis of Assissi I asked: 'Do you think anyone has such sympathy and love for birds and other creatures?' and one of the girls answered without hesitation 'Oh, yes! John Knowlittle.' ''

44 At the age of 60

Chapter XVIII

The Cruise of the "Walrus" on the Broads

"The Walrus was so named because of her broad beam, low cabin and wide stern."
A. H. PATTERSON

The "Walrus" began life as the ship's boat of "Crocus", a coalketch that foundered off the North Norfolk coast. The derelict boat, found wallowing at sea, was handed over to the Customs, the owners probably thinking her not worth the salvage money demanded. Great-grandfather paid £2 for the boat in early June 1922.

An old shrimper friend, "Chicko" Drane, towed the "Crocus" across a storm-lashed Breydon, and had to bale her out several times during the voyage to St.Olaves. In the cut called "Meen's Dyke," where "Moorhen" was moored, for some days the "Crocus" was allowed to fill and empty herself as the tides rose and fell and given opportunity to staunch her "wounds." After that, she was hauled out onto the bank, scraped inside and out, the stem and stern were tightened with galvanised wire nails and the strakes tightened with copper nails.

He engaged son-in-law Walter Saunders (my grandfather) to fit the boat out with a cabin, she was painted, varnished, a rudder added and rigged out with a little mast and sail, and the "Walrus" came into being. The interior was fitted out with settles, to sleep two, ropes, rond anchor and an awning to fling over the cockpit, cupboards and stores for comfort and domesticity.

Having shipped on board the necessary supplies, and tying aft the punt "Yarwhelp" (which was going to a new owner) and the dinghy "Florrie," they left Meen's Dyke on Thursday, 9th August at 4 p.m. a few friends wishing them "Bon Voyage." With my grandfather as skipper, the "Walrus" behaved remarkably well. They reached Breydon by nightfall and moored at great-grandfather's Breydon boatshed.

The Cruise commenced on August 10th, 1922 on the River Bure. At Acle, my grandmother met them at Wey Bridge with a basket of home-cooked food.

With the "Walrus" in the hands of his skipper, the Scribbler observed the wildlife as they toured Ranworth, St. Benet's Abbey, Potter Heigham, Hickling, Martham, Thurne and Ludham. They were entertained to lunch with friends at the White House, How Hill — a welcome change from their customary diet aboard boat of eel-stew, onions and potatoes cooked on "Lloyd George," the tin stove. They visited Barton Broad, Stalham and Salhouse, and returned to Acle from

45 Son-in-law Walter Saunders works on the conversion of the "Walrus" in Meens Dyke, St. Olaves. To his left is Edgar Blyth, Manager of the Great Yarmouth Electricity Works and the skipper of the "Moorhen" stands aboard the punt "Yarwhelp"

THE BAIT THAT DRAWS

where Patterson walked to Upton village to visit a distant relative, "Darkey" Jermany. An idling day was spent at Fleet Headquarters at St. Olaves, before the next stage of the Cruise.

They sailed up the River Yare to Berney Arms, Reedham and Brundall, from where Patterson caught a train to Norwich and spent a day browsing round the city bookshops. They explored the River Waveney, mooring at "picturesque sleepy Beccles" for one night, where harbour dues were 1/-. At Oulton Broad they met the artist T. F. Goodall, close collaborator of Dr. Peter H. Emerson on "Life and Landscape of the Norfolk Broads," and "Wildlife on a Tidal Water."

The last day of the Cruise was August 29th, and the two caught the train to Lowestoft so my grandfather could go to the Regatta and his father-in-law could visit the fishwharf.

Short notes had been kept of each day's adventures aboard the "Walrus" and though "not of a very exciting character," he admitted, "were, nevertheless, made enjoyable by the leisurely way in which the 'Walrus' crept up- and down-stream, due largely to a lack of favourable winds, and frequently none at all. The temperature was rarely summer-like, and grey skies were so constant that the freshness of the atmophere much atoned for a want of sunshine."

"The Cruise of the 'Walrus' on the Broads" published in 1923, gives an account of the conversion of the boat and subsequent cruise in the summer of 1922. The copyright of the book brought in £20. 0. 0d. The cost of the enterprise amounted to over £18. 0. 0d.

The conversion of the "Walrus" into a cabined boat had been an experiment, inasmuch as the venture was an attempt to show how a small craft could be cheaply and easily transformed into a yacht, but the experiment was unsuccessful.

"It would have been better," wrote Patterson, "had I hired a ready-made article. I was owner and commander, and like 'the wind which bloweth where it listeth,' so did I."

After the Cruise, the "Walrus" passed on to a young craftsman who gave her the refinement of a cabin with a top which would lift off so that it was possible, bent double, to stand in it, and he sailed her on the River Waveney.

Her next skipper was a schoolboy. Adding a lugsail, he sailed her in triumph across Breydon, all over the Bure, the Ant, the Thurne and back again. She later passed into other ownerships on the North River.

Finally, I am told, she came into the hands of young adventurers and sailed in races on Wroxham Broad. Dr. Daniel Shields paid £5. 0. 0d. for her, for his daughter Monica and her brother.

At the outbreak of the Second World War, the "Walrus" and other small boats were strung across Wroxham Broad as an anti-invasive measure to stop seaplanes landing there, and she did not survive. She sank in the mud at the North End of the Broad. Thus was the fate of the Good Ship "Walrus."

"The Bait that Draws"
46 Advertisement designed by Arthur Patterson for Caley's "Marching Chocolate." Featured in "The Cruise of the 'Walrus' on the Broads"

Chapter XIX

Mr. Patterson

"Late in life I became an export to Norwich." A. H. PATTERSON

After thirty-two years as a School Attendance Officer, "Old Arthur" retired on March 31st, 1926. He had by then become a highly respected and distinctive figure pottering about the town, and the kiddies called him "MR. Patt'son."

He said, in his letter of resignation:

"I beg to tender my resignation with somewhat mixed feelings. Increased years rather than wearisome of duties must be given as my excuse for retiring. I have thoroughly enjoyed my work among the humbler townsfolk and shall greatly miss the kiddies. I am glad to have seen changes . . . The schools are brighter and the children love them."

He thanked the Education Committee, Staff and Teachers, for the good understanding that had always existed between them. There had been doubts by the Chairman when he was appointed as to whether he would stick at the job. Arthur replied: "I have never yet had anything worth sticking to." His methods in the carrying out of his educational duties had been unorthordox, but had proved successful.

In the years that followed his appointment he DID stick at it and cured more boys of truanting than all the other attendance officers. He loved the boys -— though he had used his stick on them.

He recalled an incident: "When walking through George Street with a friend one Sunday noon, I espied seven sturdy lads chatting and playing on the pavement near a little mission hall. I did not know them, but they knew me.

" 'Take no notice,' I hinted to my friend, 'if these lads cut up a bit rough and rude; they mean no harm.' As we came up to them, the ringleader said 'Fall in!! 'shun!' and they did it smartly, and in the next crisp order he said 'Sal--ute!' which he and the others did prettily accompanying the action with 'Good old Patterson.' I tell you that little bit of boy-nature touched me to the quick. I knew they meant it."

The Yarmouth borough and surrounding districts raised a subscription to acknowledge Patterson's outstanding merits as a naturalist, and on his retirement a sum of £160 and an illuminated address was presented to him as "a token of their appreciation."

His letter of thanks went as follows: "May I with my wife thank you very sincerely for the great kindness shown us by Dr. Ley and yourselves. We much appreciate it. The leaves are yet green and the autumn still ahead of us, whilst winter we hope is yet a long way off. If any of you pass our way, drop in for a cup of tea, and an egg laid on the premises, and for a chat. You will be heartily welcome!"

The naturalist had made plans to move to Norwich; he considered it "the hub of Norfolk, with spikes radiating all ways."

He wrote in his diary: "Although Norfolk has only promised me a wretched 15s 6d. weekly pension, I think I can honestly say that I have (outside my family) lived to love and praise old Norfolk. I don't regret that I am not rich — unless it would have helped me to do more."

Before leaving Yarmouth, Mr. Patterson arranged an "au revoir" function among his old friends, at Johnsons' Rooms, Northgate Street. The original idea was to hold a Swan Supper, but the close season ruled *cygnus* out, so he called it "A Fraternal Feast."

47 Ibis Lodge, 197 Mill Road, Hellesdon little changed 50 years later

Menu
Soup — Breydon memories
Swan à la Patterson — roast beef ''Attmawe''
Dickey Works pudding
Houseboat potatoes
Punt cabbage
—
Moorhen pies Walrus custard
—
Burgh biscuits and North West Tower Cheese
—
Hellesdon coffee

They wished their host ''Many Happy Returns to Yarmouth!'' and they told him what they thought of him — or as much as was good for him to know! The blushes mantled to his wrinkled brow and his eye glistened with pleasure. Son Jack sang, Mr. Patterson did some of his lightning sketches and Ben Dye recited some of his poems. They reminisced about the old days on Breydon, well into the night.

At the age of seventy, my great-grandparents uprooted themselves from the environment they had always known. It proved to be a turning point in their lives. They moved to a little Elizabethan cottage in Mill Lane, Hellesdon, which they

48 A useful aid to the volume of correspondence the naturalist received

49 Leisurely days at Hellesdon, Summer 1927

named Ibis Lodge. The River Wensum was not very far away from the cottage at the bottom of the hill, and the lane led to the Golf Course, which was busy on Sundays. The cottage was described as "a dinky little place with quaint lozenge-shaped windowpanes, with new additional rooms in the rear." There was a garden at the back with potato patches and a walnut tree. At the front the cottage looked out onto a field and they were enfenced on three sides with silver birches, elms and laburnums belonging next door. There were finches and thrushes in the trees, and blue tits and starlings nested in the walnut tree. Great-grandfather built hen roosts and a duck paddock in the garden, and added aviaries and cages in which he kept jackdaws, two tawny owls and two kestrels reared from the nest.

When I visited the cottage, the field he mentioned had been replaced by a housing estate, but the cottage appeared the same as he described it.

Great-grandfather maintained wherever he went, the people would soon find he was there, and sure enough fellow-naturalists visited him or picked him up to whisk him away by car into Norfolk beauty spots.

He made plans in the winter to write biographies of the old Breydoners. He missed the mudflats — and his old Breydonside chums. Great-grandmother missed Yarmouth — and the family she had left behind.

"Christmas 1926:" great-grandfather wrote, "We old couple like Darby and Joan spent out 46th Christmas together in this quiet corner of Norfolk. The tits were with us all day and the Ducal turkey [the twentieth] given by Bedford graced the table!"

It was their last Christmas together.

Chapter XX

Mrs. Patterson

"...My wife can hold her tongue and we never talk birds, and fishes, except when the fishes smell a bit high!" A. H. PATTERSON

For a naturalist, Alice Patterson proved to be the ideal wife. She helped her husband in his natural history pursuits by not hindering him. In their early married life, when they had been extremely poor, she had not complained. She was proud of her husband, whose axiom had been "to earn my living first and provide for my family, then to abandon myself to nature and prowling."

Alice tolerated her partner's way of life — a partner who often spent nights in a boat and who came home muddy, wet and footweary. Much of his free time was spent away from home. He once said: "I would not mind living in an old tub on Breydon if I were a bachelor."

Great-grandfather was, perhaps, selfish in his principles. Yes, he provided for his wife but might he not have improved her quality of life when there were a few pence spare? She was a Paston — a distant descendant of the Medieval Pastons of Norfolk and there was talk of money "in Chancery." He would hear of no research taking place. I believe he had no desire to be rich — he had no real wish to change his life style.

A friend described great-grandmother as "homely and kind" and everyone who knew her, loved her. She was a gentlewoman — quiet, tolerant, uncomplaining. No-one but she knew her innermost feelings and thoughts — unlike her husband who penned his disappointments, frustrations, emotions.

He was not an easy man to live with and prone to bouts of temper. One day, Alice lent a caller his mackintosh as it had come on to rain heavily as he was about to leave. On her husband's return, he was so upset she had done this without his permission, he took her best hat and stamped on it!

Patterson's abstemious way of life — he neither smoked nor drank alcohol — and his outdoor pursuits toughened his constitution, for he had been far from strong as a boy. In most winters of their married life, he succumbed to bouts of influenza or chest complaints and he was not an easy patient for Mrs. Patterson to nurse. He was an active man, so felt imprisoned when confined to the house.

"Seven weeks imprisonment," he once wrote in a letter to a friend, "makes me chafe and fret like a poor linnet in a wretched little cage . . . I want to get out."

The Patterson home was shared by a multitude of strange pets from enormous snakes that escaped beneath the floorboards, to natterjack toads and frogs. Great-grandmother hated them. She tolerated the birds he brought home, either injured, or newly fledged, and those picked up by others and brought to the naturalist. There was "Joe" the cormorant who whitewashed the floor of Ibis House, a shag, and a gannet named "Jacob" who had been discovered on the south beach and brought to them in an onion sack. The gannet lodged with them for a fortnight and was fed on herring, whiting, gurnard's heads and Brazil nuts, until arrangements could be made for his removal to London Zoo. Amongst the animals there had been an otter that played with the children when there were small and sat with them by the fire to warm itself, and the white rat of their early married days which hid in places Mrs. Patterson least expected to find it!

Great-grandfather once took home a human skull and after showing it to his wife, he put it in a cupboard and went off to the marshes for the evening.

"Later on, in the stillness of the night," he recorded in his diary, "my wife was terrified to hear a rattling of dry bones in the cupboard and a steady scraping at the door. She sat petrified with fright, fully convinced that the spirit of the dead had come back to claim the

50 The Patterson Family about 1906. With their parents standing left to right Gilbert, Arthur, Helen, William, and seated John, Gerald and Alice

skull. All the time the ghastly sound went on. Luckily, I came home earlier than usual, flung open the cupboard, and out walked my pet hedgehog, bristling with indignation! He had been trying to scratch his way out."

It was not uncommon for townsfolk to call at the house at all times of the day and night with specimens for the naturalist. Anything that was curious, or out of the normal, came to the house — malformed crabs, "slinky" cods, emasculated haddocks and often Mrs. Patterson found a basket of entrails and stomach contents of cod, left overnight, on the kitchen table.

They had seven children. Their first child was a daughter — Alice (known as Jessie), then came two sons Arthur and William, then my grandmother, Helen (known as Nellie), Gilbert, John (known as Jack) and Gerald. The five boys fought

51 The Scribbler in his "den" at Ibis House

in the First World War: two of them came home wounded and, like many mothers, Mrs. Patterson suffered the heartbreak of losing a son — Gerald, killed in France in 1916. My grandmother worked as a milliner in the store in which her father was employed as warehouseman.

When great-grandfather was at home, he needed a private place away from the exuberance of his large family, so the front room served as his "Den" or "Workshop." He took all his meals there. The room was sacred — and typical of a naturalist's study. His desk was never able to cope with all his papers, so they overflowed onto several tables and most of the chairs. A mixture of baskets, specimen cases and butterfly nets filled up the corners of the room. A huge bookcase filled one side of the room to house his 500 "hobby books" on birds, fishing, poaching and so on, and an aquarium or vivarium housed some form of animal life. This stood in the bay window. The walls contained works of the artists Charles Harrison, Stephen Batchelder, Frank Southgate and Roland Green, and there were framed photographs of his boats. The only stuffed bird was a Java dove, which had been a pet for 30 years.

For many years great-grandfather paid for the keep of a grandson fostered by a family at Acle, Norfolk. During the school holidays he stayed with his grandparents at Ibis House. Whilst the naturalist was out one day, Herbert, unbeknown to his grandmother, fished for "tiddlers" in the aquarium in his grandfather's study. They were, in fact, rare fish he was breeding! On grandfather's return home, he chased Herbert down the street, and caught him. The Truant Officer was a good runner and used to catching naughty boys. Herbert remembers the hiding he received to this day.

"Weddun's ain't my scene," great-grandfather once said. He hated social occasions and luncheons because, he said: "My one tooth doesn't shine at feasts!" However, when Herbert and his sweetheart Lilian invited him to their wedding, to the great surprise of everyone he accepted. It was the first — and the last — wedding he attended since his own in 1880.

Herbert told me about his wedding day. The parson did not turn up — he had mistaken the date and gone off to a garden party! Great-grandfather was furious and rapped on the vestry door with his stick until the verger, in a state of embarrassment and perspiration, appeared. By the time the parson was found, it was too late in the day for the marriage to take place. But the reception proceeded with toasts to "The Bride and Groom to Be" and "The Bridesmaids to Be". (The ceremony took place the following day.)

He was most persistent if he wanted anything and had his serious likes and dislikes. He also knew WHAT he wanted.

He had always wished for a great-grandson. When a daughter was born to Herbert and Lilian at Caister, proud father cycled the couple of miles to Yarmouth to tell him the good news. They met on Lichfield Road. Great-grandfather said: "Well, what is it?" "A daughter," Herbert replied, and with that he walked off without a word. He did, however, grow to like his little great-granddaughter Ann.

The Patterson name has gone now — his sons had daughters and ironically it was the daughters who produced grandsons for him. My father, Howard Saunders, his second grandson, spent his holidays at Ibis House. On the occasion of his 10th birthday his mother was away in Liverpool and I found a letter he wrote her which describes "a day with Grandma."

In later life, my great-grandmother, who was of Primitive Methodist ancestry, and whose brother had entered the ministry, became a Congregationalist and was a member of the King Street Church, Yarmouth. By profession, she was an elocutionist, but in 1912, the operation to the throat left her with a husky voice. She

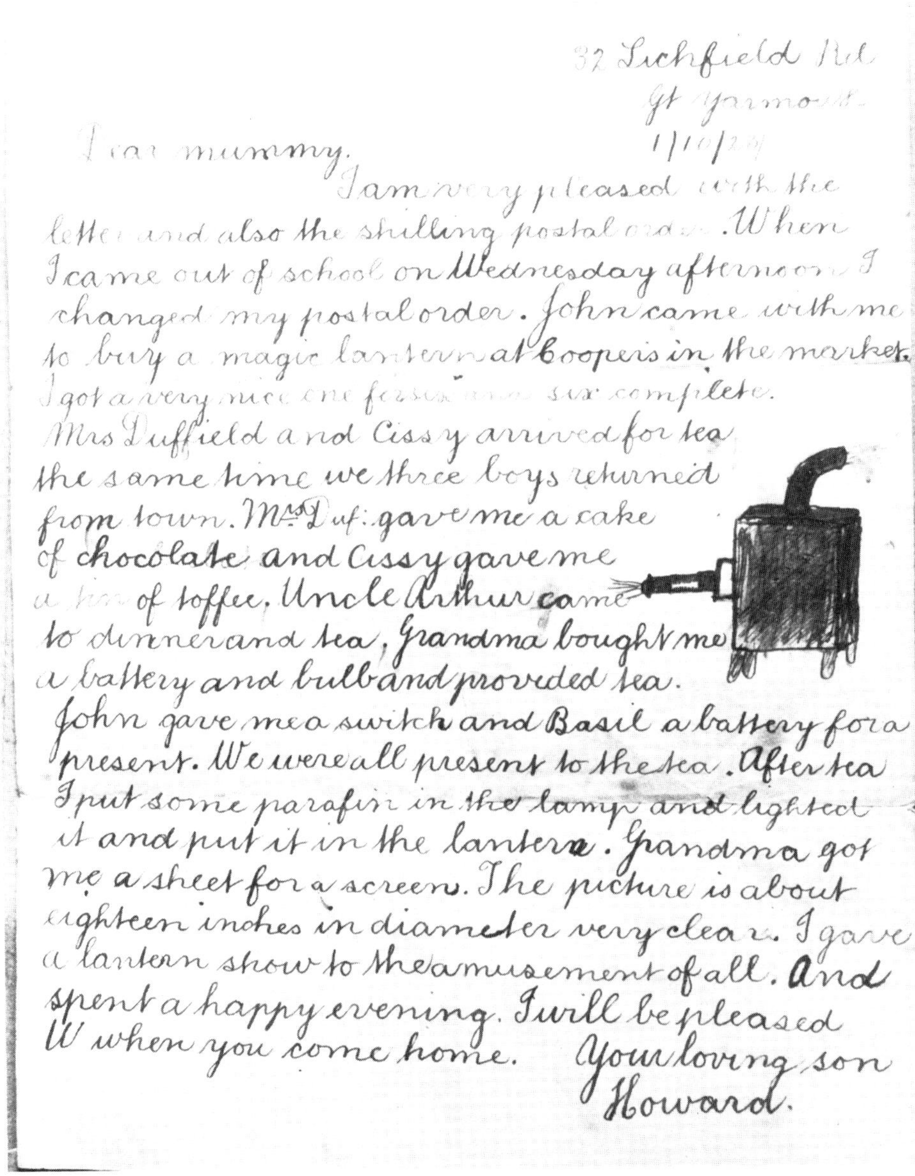

32 Lichfield Rd
Gt Yarmouth
1/10/24

Dear mummy.
I am very pleased with the letter and also the shilling postal order. When I came out of school on Wednesday afternoon I changed my postal order. John came with me to buy a magic lantern at Cooper's in the market. I got a very nice one for six and six complete. Mrs Duffield and Cissy arrived for tea the same time we three boys returned from town. Mrs Duf: gave me a cake of chocolate and Cissy gave me a tin of toffee. Uncle Arthur came to dinner and tea, Grandma bought me a battery and bulb and provided tea. John gave me a switch and Basil a battery for a present. We were all present to the tea. After tea I put some parafin in the lamp and lighted it and put it in the lantern. Grandma got me a sheet for a screen. The picture is about eighteen inches in diameter very clear. I gave a lantern show to the amusement of all. And spent a happy evening. I will be pleased when you come home. Your loving son
Howard.

52 Letter written by Howard Patterson Saunders at the age of 10

was gifted with a retentive memory, and in middle years became a reciter, visiting the workhouse, mothers' meetings and similar gatherings to entertain with poems —dramatic, pathetic and humorous.

On February 14th, 1927, the quiet, happy, well-earned home of retirement at Hellesdon became a house of sorrow. Alice, Patterson's dear old partner of forty-six years and chum of nearly sixty years, after a brief illness, passed peacefully away with nearly all her children round her. She was 70. My great-grandmother left a memory to be treasured by those who knew and loved her.

Great-grandfather was devastated. In his diary, he pasted this picture of her and wrote:

53 On the beach with daughter Nellie and grandson Howard seated centre

"Alice Elizabeth Paston
born 10.12.57
became my sweetheart 1868
married 5.2.81
Died — as she lived — splendid
The saddest event of my life."

Townsfolk joined family and friends at her funeral at Gorleston Cemetery where she was buried next to the Paston family grave. Great-grandfather — distraught and heartbroken — was not well enough to attend.

My grandmother, who had lived at Ibis House while her parents were at Hellesdon, took charge of her father and accompanied him back to Yarmouth to look after him. In a letter to his friend Fred Cook, he wrote:

"Thanks for your kind sympathy. I feel very lonely especially when in my room alone. I've got all my books round me and I hope to break the monotony of tears by scribbling another book . . . I'm settled again, as afore."

54 This photograph of Alice standing by the door of Ibis Lodge was pasted in Arthur Patterson's diary on the occasion of her death on St. Valentine's Day, 1927. He wrote below it:

"Alice Elizabeth Paston born 10.12. 57, became my sweetheart, 1868 married 5.2.81. Died—as she lived—splendid:

The saddest event of my life"

55 Edward (Ted) Ellis at Keswick Hall about 1927

Chapter XXI

The Writer

"... Young Ellis hath eyes of a falcon and the optimism of a Sancho Panza."
A. H. PATTERSON

Before moving to Hellesdon, great-grandfather made the acquaintance of a young boy named Edward A. Ellis. Ted had become a naturalist at a very early age in his native Guernsey and after the War his parents moved to Gorleston. One day Ted and his younger brother Martin cycled to Yarmouth to introduce themselves to

56 Taken on an excursion to Horning, Norfolk in 1927

Mr. Patterson. The naturalist, who by then was over 60, welcomed in the two boys and encouraged then to keep nature diaries as he had been doing for forty years.

Patterson found comfort in Ted, who was a bright boy, with an enquiring mind. He still mourned for his naturalist son Gerald and the boy filled a gap in his life. When Ted left school, great-grandfather secured for the young naturalist a job as Keeper of Foreign Birds for Gerard Gurney at Keswick Hall, near Norwich. Ted visited the Pattersons often whilst they were living at Hellesdon.

Ted left Keswick Hall in July 1927, (by which time Patterson was back at Yarmouth) and for a year, was between jobs with, consequently, a good deal of spare time. A strong friendship developed between the two naturalists.

They rambled together and Patterson was impressed at his friend's ability to name all the plants and butterflies they saw. Ted stayed with him on the houseboat

57 Dictating "Nights and Days" renamed "Wildfowlers and Poachers" to Ted Ellis at Ibis House

and went to Ibis House on Saturday nights for a "mardle." Patterson was working on his latest book "Wildfowlers and Poachers" at the time and Ted typed the manuscript for him.

On November 16th, 1927, Ted Ellis made his first public appearance — the forerunner of many. It was at the Rotary Club Meeting at Arnolds Restaurant, Yarmouth, and he gave a talk entitled "Some Delights of a Young Naturalist."

Patterson urged Ted to apply for the post of naturalist at the Castle Museum, Norwich and in November 1928, he was appointed. He was there for 28 years. Over the years, his good-natured, easy-going manner has earned him a place in the hearts of all those interested in the World of Nature. Through television his face is well-known and he is a popular speaker — pulling in the crowds — at natural history meetings, presentations, fetes, and so on. His greatest honour came in June

58 With Harry Hurrell, Manager of the "Eastern Daily Press" Yarmouth office September 8th, 1931

1970 (Wildlife Conservation Year), when he was conferred Honorary Doctor of Science by the University of East Anglia. Self-taught — he admits Arthur Patterson had a great influence on his life.

During that November meeting in 1927 it was proposed another meeting be called with a view to relaunching the Yarmouth Naturalists' Society. The former minute books were found and a week later, at a public meeting at Johnsons' Rooms, Northgate Street, the Society was reformed. (It was the fourth society of its kind —the first was set up in 1830, the second in 1889-1891, and the third, a Yarmouth Branch of the Norfolk and Norwich Naturalists' Society, in 1893).

Harry Hurrell, manager of the Eastern Daily Press Office at Yarmouth, who

59 Third Ramble of reformed Great Yarmouth Naturalists' Society in August 1928 to Mautby and West Caister. Left to right Arthur Patterson (barely visible), Howard Saunders, Helen Saunders, Phillip Rumbelow, Ben Dye and Murray Simpson

had an especial interest in the study of minute aquatic life of Breydon Water, the Broads and the coast, was elected Chairman, with Patterson as vice-chairman and D. Drummond and Ted Ellis as joint-secretaries.

The field meetings of the newly formed society were recorded by Philip Rumbelow, the Yarmouth naturalist, in his dairy of 1928. The first outing was to Belton, Fritton and St.Olaves; the second to Hopton and Lound; and the third to Mautby and West Caister. The date of the latter Saturday, August 25th happened to coincide with the opening of the football season, so only a dozen turned up for the ramble. My grandmother and father were amongst them. Rumbelow provided everyone with a booklet describing the route and included a map which added much to the pleasure of the walk. They examined flora, there was a good show of Peacock, Small Tortoiseshell, Small Copper and Painted Lady butterflies plus a female Clouded Yellow, and the larva of the Great Elephant Hawkmoth. They viewed Caister Castle, and the ruined church of St. Edmund, later returning to Yarmouth by tram.

"Wildfowlers and Poachers" was published in March 1929. Patterson had

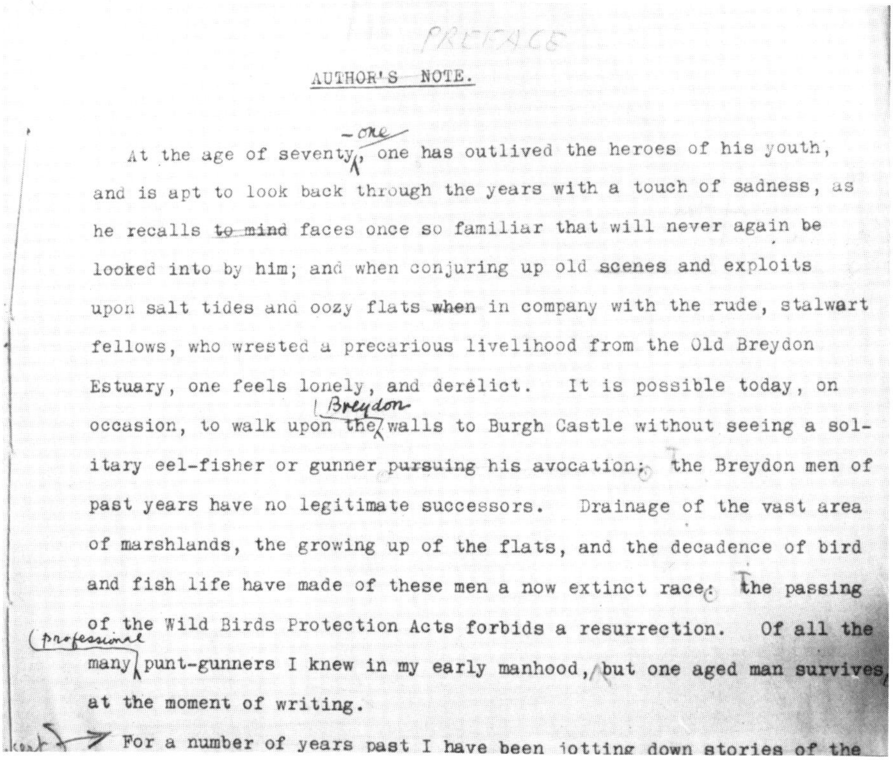

PREFACE

AUTHOR'S NOTE.

At the age of seventy-one, one has outlived the heroes of his youth, and is apt to look back through the years with a touch of sadness, as he recalls ~~to mind~~ faces once so familiar that will never again be looked into by him; and when conjuring up old scenes and exploits upon salt tides and oozy flats when in company with the rude, stalwart fellows, who wrested a precarious livelihood from the Old Breydon Estuary, one feels lonely, and derelict. It is possible today, on occasion, to walk upon ~~the~~ Breydon walls to Burgh Castle without seeing a solitary eel-fisher or gunner pursuing his avocation; the Breydon men of past years have no legitimate successors. Drainage of the vast area of marshlands, the growing up of the flats, and the decadence of bird and fish life have made of these men a now extinct race; the passing of the Wild Birds Protection Acts forbids a resurrection. Of all the many professional punt-gunners I knew in my early manhood, but one aged man survives, at the moment of writing.

For a number of years past I have been jotting down stories of the

60 Corrected proof copy of preface to "Wildfowlers and Poachers"

begun the book towards the end of the War "to while away the hours" when mourning the loss of his son. He had named it "The Snipe Shooters Club." A second attempt was made in 1925 which he called "Wildfowlers Arms and Snipe Shooters Club," but he destroyed the manuscript before returning to Yarmouth in 1927.

He dedicated the book to the memory of his wife and beloved Norfolk.

It had been, he wrote, "a 20 year project — my last testament of Breydon — those I knew as a lad — eelers, smelters, walking gunners, wildfowlers, poachers."

In the preface he wrote the words of Robert Burns:

"A gentle curlew bidding kind goodnight."

In reminiscent mood in the same year, Patterson wrote a series of articles for the "Eastern Daily Press" about "Life in the Sixties and Seventies," covering subjects like "The Chair Mender," "Childrens' Toys," and "Old Time Street Musicians."

"The period of the Sixties," he said, "afforded me much pleasant rumination for there

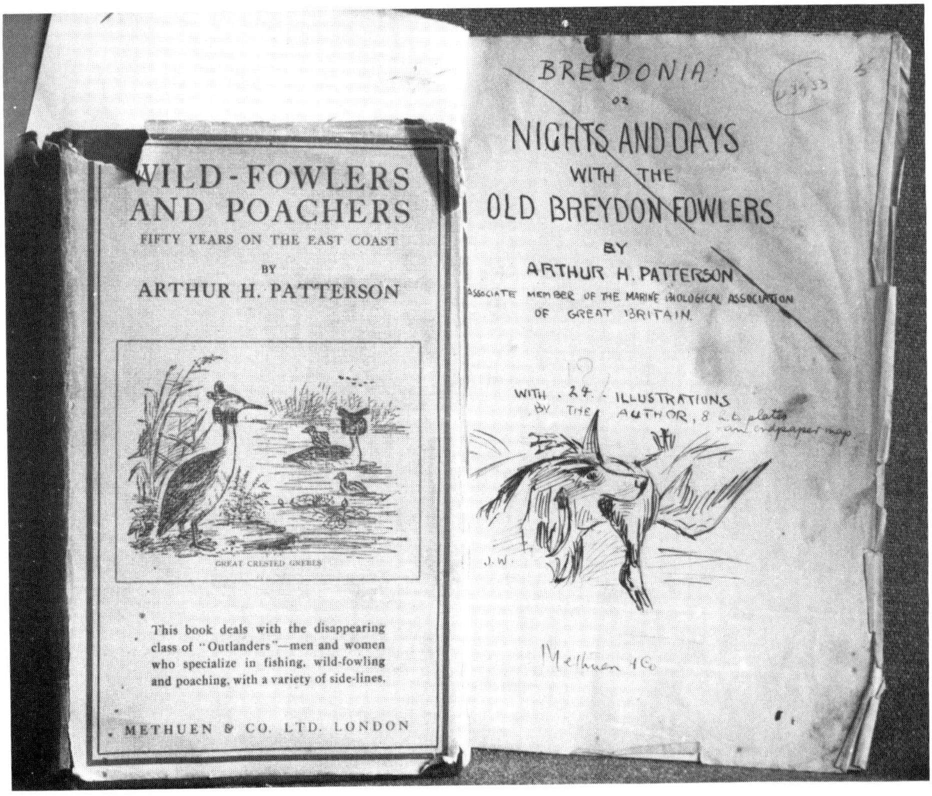

61 Original proof title page and dust cover of "Wildfowlers and Poachers"

was still an old worldness that subsequent decades have uprooted, overrun and obliterated."

Three books were published in 1930. A selection of observations of birds, mammals and fish from 23 diaries was published in "A Norfolk Naturalist." The "Times Literary Supplement" said in their review of the book " . . . the observation is both comprehensive and acute, the description simple and direct without any applied ornament . . .", whilst "The Observer" put the book "in the class of White's 'Natural History and Antiquity of Selborne' " first published in 1789.

An imaginative work entitled "In Norfolk Bird Haunts in A.D.1755" endeavoured to portray Breydon as it appeared in the middle of the 18th century, using Old Joe Thomas (an 18th century wildfowler) and Sylas Neville (a contemporary diarist) as models for the characters "Harnser Smith" (Breydon fowler) and "Sylas Hardley" (Cockney naturalist) respectively. The original title "Breydon Wildfowlers of A.D.1755" had been changed by the publishers owing to its similarity to his "Wildfowlers and Poachers."

"Through Broadland by Sail and Motor" followed an extensive race round the Broads and rivers during a week in July 1929, in a Blake's motorised yacht "Harmony" skippered again by my grandfather. It was dedicated to the Broadland pioneers Ernest Suffling and G. Christopher Davies, (author of "The Swan and her Crew" a book which was a decided stimulus to Patterson's love of Broadland and a taste for adventure in a boat).

It was the last book Arthur Patterson wrote. He was 73 and, although he continued to scribble, did not embark on any further extensive works. He had over the years written, along with hundreds of articles for newspapers, periodicals, leaflets and reports to natural history organisations, 26 books.

He owed, he said, "a debt to Defoe for his plain, clear English, added to that of the Old Testament, have helped me to a choicer language than my Breydon companionship might warrant." He further added "a big well-marked but not mutilated Bible and a concordance [an alphabetical register of words, usually Biblical, used by an author] stand side by side with a dictionary on one especial shelf in my library, which volumes I refer to as my 'literary planes and chisels.' "

Arthur Patterson used beautiful sentences to place in his books and scribblings from writers like Thoreau, Emerson, E. L. Turner, Mark Twain, and his patron saint "Robinson Crusoe" who, he said "made a Broadlander of me." Arthur Smith, one of his greatest friends, said of him: "His cheerful effortless work was like fireside gossip. He never struggled to round a sentence or polish a phrase. Having something to say, he said it, in the way of one who wished his readers to understand."

"However small the query," said "Ejector" of the "Eastern Daily Press," "his queries were always courteous and authentic, more often than not accompanied with one of his inimitable and life-like illustrations." He made a habit of scribbling cartoons on the envelopes to friends and the Post Office staff was said to have held back his post at the sorting office, so that the next shift might see and enjoy them too! He was a rapid writer . . . "with a peculiar caligraphy only to be read easily by those familiar with its quaint whirls and spidery curls," it was said.

The Patterson collection represented the labour of a naturalist's lifetime and after he died, it was said: "He has left a legacy to the literature of Norfolk books showing mastery of his chosen fields, all distinguished by clear, incisive writing."

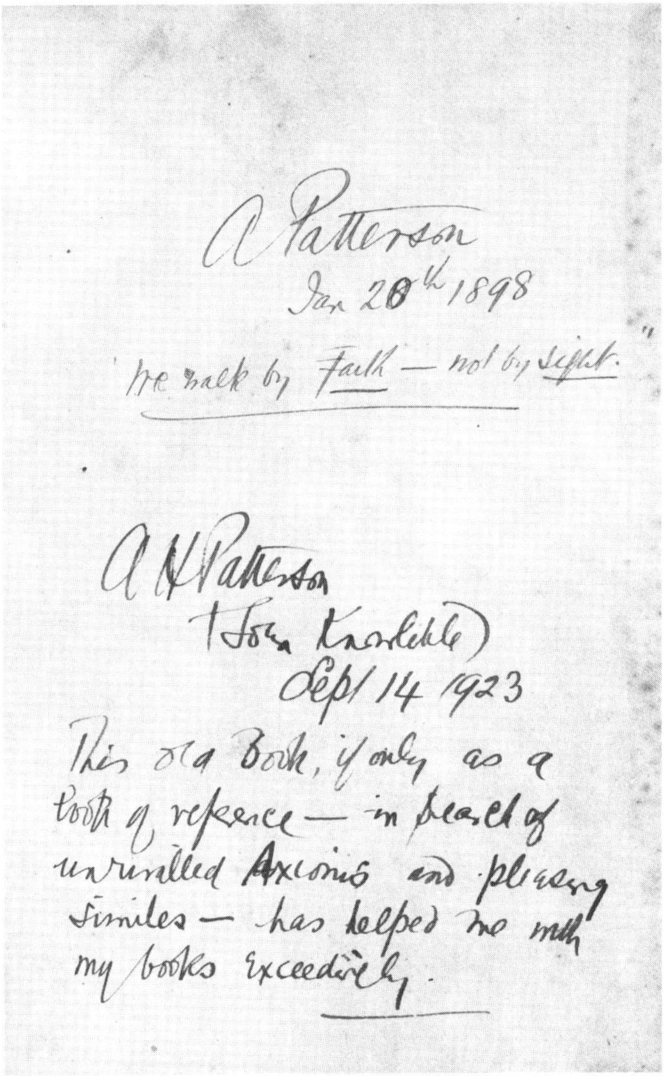
A Patterson
Jan 20th 1898
"We walk by Faith — not by Sight."

A H Patterson
(John Knowlittle)
Sept 14 1923
This old Book, if only as a book of reference — in search of unrivalled Axioms and pleasing similes — has helped me with my books exceedingly.

62 Flysheet of Arthur Patterson's bible

Chapter XXII

"Barbarian of the Broads"

"Everyone should have a hobby to counterbalance the necessities of work. From my childhood everything living had an interest for me and tempted me into the open and lone places . . ." —A. H. PATTERSON

As a School Attendance Officer great-grandfather enjoyed long holidays in the summer and took the oportunity to take trips into Broadland in his boats. His adventures were enjoyed by hundreds of people who read his nature notes and articles in the "Eastern Daily Press." He wanted others to be aware that nature was always fresh and interesting.

He was happy aboard the houseboat and admitted he could look like a tramp. He detested smart clothes and never felt free and easy in a decent suit.

In the winter of 1912 the naturalist acquired an old punt to be used for the bottom of a new houseboat. By this time, the "Moorhen" was just about "done

63 Lazy days at St. Olaves with daughter Helen and friends

for,'' he said. At the age of 74 his lifelong chum Ben Harwood built ''Moorhen II.'' She was launched on May 24th, 1913, and taken to Meen's Dyke, St.Olaves where ''she was moored in a quiet cutting, out of the way of traffic. There was a good dry bank and the 'hanger' at the rear of the pretty little farm [belonging to Lenny Meen] was heatherclad and adorned by fir trees, whilst the marshland stretched away to a far horizon on the frontage.''

St.Olaves became his base for several years. From his home the naturalist could reach the village easily by train (the passenger service came to an end on November

64 At Belton Fen with Tom Brooks, carpenter and wheelright. On the 3½ acre fen he kept fowls and bees and grew vegetables. The photographer stated: ''They were in ernest conversation over the location of a nest and completely unaware of the presence of a camera.'' August 1931. His nephew Oliver ''Franie'' Brooks was ''the young urchin'' in Patterson's ''Wildlife on a Norfolk Estuary,'' worked as a marshman till well into his seventies and lives on the edge of Burgh Castle marshes today

2nd, 1959) and he barrowed his provisions along the track to the cutting. Friends popped in from time to time and the family visited him.

The houseboat was fitted out with settles, with room below for stowage, cupboards, lockers, a fireplace and a table. There were paintings on the wall and a bookcase held favourite books like Thoreau's ''Concord'' and ''Malden.'' There were pickle bottles for specimens, pens and ample supply of writing paper. Outside were his fishing rods, eel-pick and eel-trunk.

In the summer of 1919, he revisited Broadland in the punt ''Yarwhelp''.

65 ''Moorhen II''

66 "Bed-time afloat" An illustration from "Through Broadland in a Breydon Punt" Aboard "Yarwhelp" near the Malthouse, Oulton Broad

He had the punt fitted out "to make her a sleeping hut on an exhaustive trip on Broadland waters. So I can sail her by day and roost at night," he said. "It'll be a tight fit, but one looks for fine weather in August holidays." The punt was, he described: "High apeak, difficult in a wind, loving to make leeway, but she was as comfortable as a hammock — just suitable for a crank." He used a tin stove on which to cook his food which he called "Lloyd George" because, he admitted, "it soon gets warmed up and the onlookers know it!"

He wrote a daily account of his experiences for the "Eastern Daily Press" and the following year a book telling the story of the trip was published. It was called "Through Broadland in a Breydon Punt."

In the summer of 1921 "Broadland's famous author amongst his feathered and finny friends" was featured in the "Eastern Daily Press" with "Holiday Nights and Days on Breydon." He stayed with George Jary, the Breydon Watcher, aboard his houseboat.

With the peculiar aptness displayed by the Norfolk natives for bestowing at once an expressive nickname, George had immediately been called "New-come" Jary, a name which stuck all his life. He was the second "Watcher" to be appointed by the Breydon Protection Committee, administered by the Great Yarmouth Naturalists' Society and the sly visits of the more daring defiers of the law ceased.

67 Rowing a punt on Breydon in 1921

Jary's houseboat was moored in a small creek near the Ship Drain on Breydon.

"She is no beauty — this ark," Patterson wrote, "and never was, for which sane boatbuilder would waste his arts or pains on an iron-fastened hull, not a new one at that, when this cabin was erected above it. After eighteen years of roughing it on this wild estuary, she has grown 'nail-sick' . . ."

He nicknamed the houseboat "Pickle-tub" — rather aptly, perhaps, because of its contents and the daily bucket of salt water that percolated between the aged timbers. They were at the ship's pumps daily.

"Moorhen III" was launched early in the summer of 1930. Patterson engaged Harry "Ikey" Smith, a marshman-naturalist to build a hut on top of a small sailing

68 George Jary, the Breydon Birdwatcher, 1927

69 On Breydon south wall in September 1930. This picture was reproduced as Christmas cards the following year

boat brought from my grandfather when he became too ill to sail it himself. Smith was a skilled taxidermist, mechanic and built himself a typical Norfolk gun-punt. He lived at Three Mile House, an isolated marsh farm by the River Bure.

The new houseboat was taken up river to join a small fleet of houseboats at Acle dyke, near Eastick's boatyard, one of which belonged to Edgar Bligh, manager of the Electricity Works on the Yarmouth Denes. [Bligh saved the naturalist marine specimens trapped in the filters.] "Moorhen III" provided great-grandfather with

70 "What time is high water?" illustration from "Wildfowlers and Poachers." It is taken outside Ibis House in 1928. Arthur Patterson is wearing carpet slippers and on his watch chain are the marks of a Showman—two tiger claws

sleeping quarters and a place to entertain friends.

Early in 1933, "Moorhen III" was moved to St.Olaves where he and son William sawed in half the old houseboat "Moorhen II" and reconstituted half ashore for a cook- and stowage-house, and smashed the other half up.

At the end of the year, great-grandfather caught a chill after a car-ride to Cley-next-the-Sea. He was flooded with good wishes, which he acknowledged by sending out nearly one hundred photographs of himself standing on the south Breydon wall.

From photographs of Arthur Patterson, it would appear he was always "properly dressed," and the fact that he wore a "dickey-front" (a stiffened cotton

71 "Making a note on Breydon" with Bull-death the Breydon Watcher

shirt-front with attached collar and tie) probably accounts for this appearance. A former employee of his friend Fred Cook told me great-grandfather visited the tailor's shop one day clutching a dickey-front and apologising profusely for being incorrectly dressed, only to discover when it was pointed out to him, he was already wearing one! He always wore a waistcoat and from his watch-chain hung the "charms" of a showman — two tiger claws.

He could be most fastidious especially when he was the subject of a photograph. Evelyn Weston, a journalist, who acknowledged that Arthur Patterson "started me off on the inky way" took a photograph of him in the early Thirties. It is featured in "Wildfowlers and Poachers" captioned "What Time is high water?" She wrote the following in an article in "The Field" just after his death. "It was taken outside the gate of Ibis House," she said, "and the taking of it was rather a riot. He first of all held up the proceedings while he polished the brass plate beside the door; then he thought he would rather wear a different hat, so went in to change, and when the photograph was finally taken, developed and printed, I discovered he was wearing his bedroom slippers."

Great-grandfather was at his happiest "Up Breydon" or as, in his own words, "Barbarian of the Broads."

72 ''Barbarian of the Broads''—aboard ''Moorhen I'' July 1907

74 Caricature of John Knowlittle by Matt, featured in the "Sunday Graphic"

Chapter XXIII

The Last (Swan) Supper

"Each muster revealed the passing of many of the 'old crew'." . . . A. H. PATTERSON

In January 1934 great-grandfather invited several Breydon wildfowlers and naturalists to a Swan Supper, the fourth to be held in twenty years. The venue was Johnsons Rooms, in Northgate Street and each was given a menu card decorated with sketches by him. After supper until late in the evening they recalled memories of Breydon and Breydoners "Mussle", "Pintle", "Gabey" and "Gut" Thomas, "Silky" Watson, "Fiddler" Goodens, Pero Pestell, Jimmy Hurr, the Thackers, the Sharmans and "Admiral" Gooch. It was to be the last Breydoners' Swan Supper.

Patterson had, at the age of 76, himself seen many of his Breydon chums pass over to "The Great Divide" and so he wrote a series of articles for the "Eastern Daily Press" — 29 in all — on "Some Old Yarmouth Sportsmen."

"By bringing these chapters dealing with Breydon men, both rich and poor, to a close,"he said, "it seems like bidding a second goodbye to a lot of old friends." (His first testament to the Breydon fraternity had been his "Wildfowlers and Poachers.")

From the houseboat at St.Olaves, the naturalist explored the Lothingland district, met friends and continued to promote the welfare of birds. Matt the cartoonist featured John Knowlittle in the "Sunday Graphic" and "Sunday News" and caught J.K.'s little frown wonderfully well.

"Am much troubled with rheumatism . . . am now hoping to get back again soon to Breydon."

The naturalist wrote these words in his diary in March 1935. He was 77 and becoming frail. When approached by the "British Broadcasting Corporation" to give a radio broadcast he declined the offer — said age was against his travelling to London and that he felt unable to undergo the ordeal of facing the microphone.

Arthur Patterson had known Breydon Water in its heyday. In 1896 he observed effects of drainage operations and other processes which were causing the marshes to become dry and Breydon to "grow up" in such a way that a smaller area of mudflats was covered at high tide. At that time in a letter to the "Eastern Daily Press" he urged that, as acres of Breydon were useless even to the wildfowler, it should be dredged. This, he considered, could have a) formed a better basin for reception of tides, b) the fowler would grumble less, and c) mussels could have been farmed there by the Breydoners on a cooperative basis.

His suggestions were not implemented and several years later when asked "What can we do with Breydon?" the Breydon naturalist replied "Let it alone."

On May 9th, 1935, Arthur Patterson was elected an Associate of the Linnean Society of London. He had realised his ambition. He was recognised at last and was delighted. Congratulations flooded in — including one from the Duchess of Bedford who had put forward his name in 1906.

"I congratulate you on getting the A.L.S. at last." she wrote. "It is rather a pity they wait quite so long to give these awards as they would be more appreciated when one is a little younger. However, I know you have waited for it a long time, and 'better late than never!' " He had, indeed, waited a long time — 29 years.

In the summer he visited Norwich, but was overcome by the heat and caught an early train home. He visited the fishwharf at Lowestoft, but it depressed him to see unemployed men standing idle at the wharf gate. Fishing by 1935 had become a sadly dwindling occupation — Patterson had known the industry in its heyday. He visited Breydon for the last time.

On July 23rd he fell down the stairs of the Yarmouth Mercury Office from top to bottom. He suffered injuries to his head and face and was severely shaken by the fall. "His face," wrote a friend, "was a shocking sight, but he stood up to his bumping well without doing himself any serious injury." He made very slow progress to recovery, but grew thin owing to the fact he couldn't eat any solid food. After three weeks, he went to stay at his son John's home to give my grandmother, who had been his housekeeper since great-grandmother died, a rest.

"First note since my fall." he recorded in his diary in August. "A fall downstairs and three weeks — so far — mostly in bed — have rusted my pen a bit."

73 With friend Fred Cook at Oulton Broad in 1934

He sent for Fred Cook to visit him, who said he was looking very ill when he called at Ibis House on August 18th.

Diary entry: "20.8.35 - SPECIAL:

"My illness has kept me from even the smell of Breydon, but a smart young naturalist from Hereford, who, having read one or two of my books, biked over to see, if possible, an avocet. Strangely enough 16 visited us from Breydon. He was delighted to see more at ONE TIME than ever I had. There were several godwits about at the time and some knots. This young fellow is a born naturalist, cool, careful, and appreciative. He had his binoculars at his side, and made good use of it. He has just gone off on his bike . . ."

It was the last entry great-grandfather wrote in his diary. His health continued to deteriorate and his memory began to fail him. After a fall at home, his mind

75 The once thriving Bowling Green tavern in a state of dereliction, February 1930

became more and more troubled, and he was admitted to Northgate Hospital, 150A Caister Road, Great Yarmouth.

As the delusions lessened, so his mind became more normal, but he grew weaker and weaker until, recognising no-one, he drifted into unconsciousness. Without regaining consciousness he had a peaceful end on Sunday October 27th, 1935 at 11.15 a.m. Arthur Patterson had finally laid down his pen!

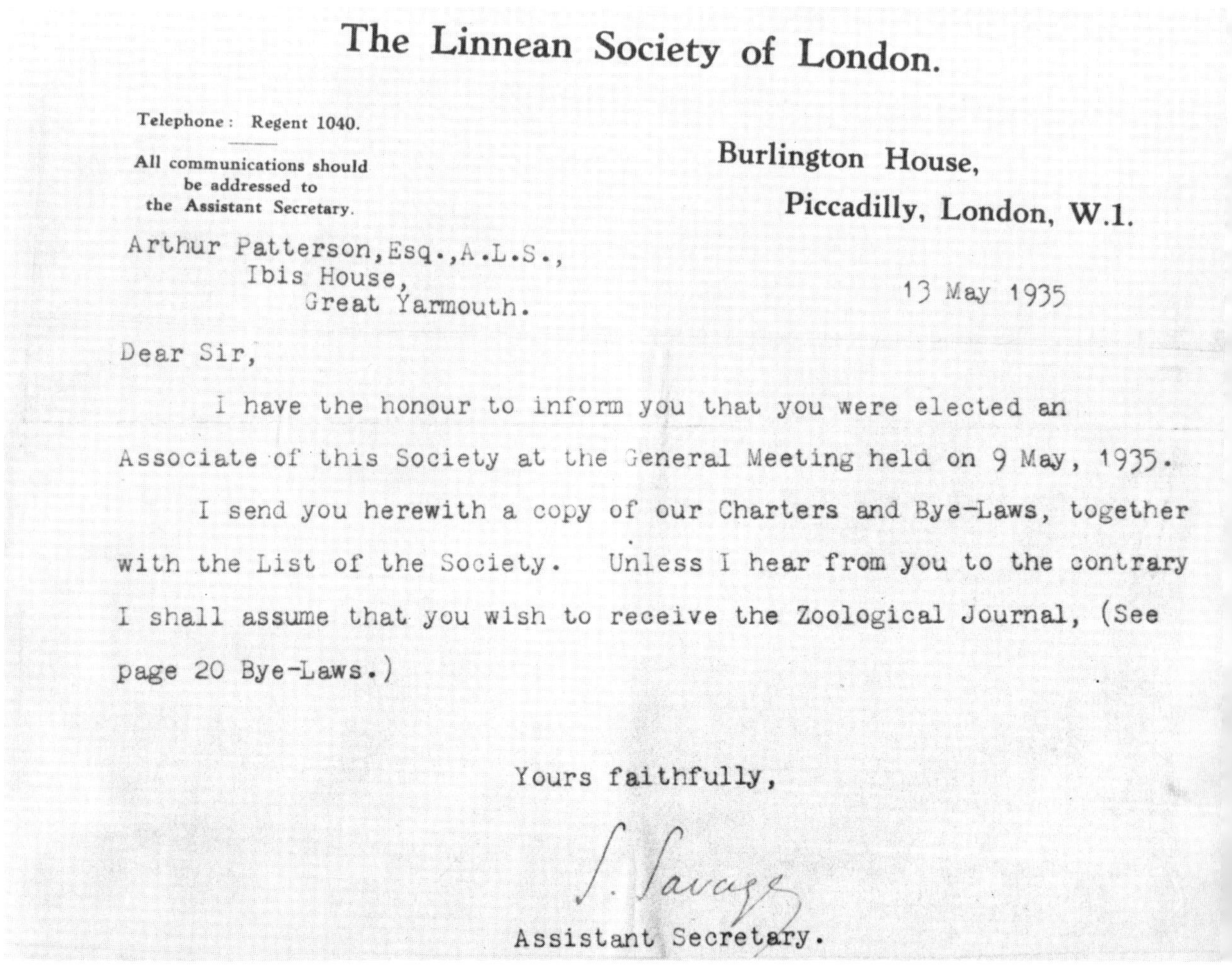

The Linnean Society of London.

Telephone: Regent 1040.

All communications should be addressed to the Assistant Secretary.

Burlington House,
Piccadilly, London, W.1.

Arthur Patterson, Esq., A.L.S.,
Ibis House,
Great Yarmouth.

13 May 1935

Dear Sir,

I have the honour to inform you that you were elected an Associate of this Society at the General Meeting held on 9 May, 1935.

I send you herewith a copy of our Charters and Bye-Laws, together with the List of the Society. Unless I hear from you to the contrary I shall assume that you wish to receive the Zoological Journal, (See page 20 Bye-Laws.)

Yours faithfully,

S. Savage

Assistant Secretary.

76 Recognition at last for Arthur Patterson

Chapter XXIV

The Boy from the "Rows"

> "I do not suppose I have accomplished anything unusual or noteworthy but I have derived immense pleasure from my pursuit of nature. Had my opportunities and worldly circumstances been less enviable, I might have done better. As it is, I have done my best."
>
> A. H. PATTERSON

"All the education I got was under Wallis," Arthur Patterson once said, "the polish I got afterwards by years of grind."

William Wallis was a great influence on the small boy from the "Rows." He introduced him to the countryside and taught him to appreciate the wildlife and flowers. He recognised his flair for art and his natural ability to entertain and employed him to draw on the blackboard to amuse the other children. It was a poor school with very few books. Arthur had to learn the names of the wild creatures from the bird-catchers and fisherfolk and became exasperated when he learned later they had been local names and scientifically incorrect.

His childhood in the Yarmouth Rows was a sad one. He lost his mother at an early age and one by one his brothers and sisters died until he was an only child. His new stepmother was unused to children and was a strict disciplinarian, but I think she liked the boy. She bought him comics with natural history articles in them and took him to the Circus and Menagerie when they came to Town. How he loved the smell of the animals and the excitement of Yarmouth Fair — "the blare of gongs and clash of bells," he remembered years later, "the yell of rival 'doorsmen' and a wheezy barrel organ.." The life a showman led fascinated him.

William Patterson never could "fathom him out" and called his roaming about "idling about" but the boy was very stubborn and determined to excel as a naturalist in spite of his father's protestations. He smuggled home pets — white mice, rats, guinea pigs, silkworms, a tortoise and kept them in secret places. He idolised the cats that swarmed in the Rows. Undoubtedly they brought him comfort, for his parents were unable to show physical love.

He was not a strong child. All through his life he suffered chest complaints and when confined to bed admitted to being "an unwilling prisoner." He had the opportunity of a job at Regents Park Zoo, London but had to turn it down as the doctor thought the atmosphere would be bad for his health.

The second biggest influence on his life came from his acquaintance with a Breydoner named Ben Harwood who became a life-long friend. He was quite a bit older than Arthur and experienced in all the things that fascinated him — punting on Breydon, fishing, "picking" for eels and shooting.

Arthur had a variety of jobs. First he was a Pupil Teacher under Wallis, then he became an Assurance Agent. He was a relief postman and a Pedlar. He said he "dreamed peddling and could comprehend what the wolf at the door meant." His spare hours were spent bird-stuffing to barter for books and later he scribbled notes for the paper and to pay for his boat and boatshed. In 1880 he wrote to J. H. Gurney asking if he knew of employment in natural history but he was told there were more applicants than posts. Twice he left Yarmouth to take up posts in Zoos, and although he gained useful experience in the keeping of foreign animals and wrote books on the subject, the work did not suit him and on his return home found himself unemployed and very nearly penniless. But he was a great optimist and sought out work. He hated being idle. He printed grocers' tickets, caught and sold fish, worked his "shadowgraph" in schools and was a Showman. When needing new boots he obtained a pair in a most original way:

He wrote in his diary,

"I have for years used Freeman Hardy and Willis Army "Bluchers." The manager of one of their branches offered to exchange a pair of new tan boots for my old nearly worn out ones, providing they were allowed to be exhibited as an advert in his window. I consented.

> 'This pair of Army Bluchers — our own make were worn by Arthur Patterson (The Yarmouth Naturalist). They have carried their owner many a score mile by seashore, riverside and road. He says "They are the most comfortable boots in existence.' "

"Audacity is often a trump card to a naturalist!" he maintained.

"I have had my ups and downs," he said, "but I do not entertain one solitary grudge against fate." When in his thirties and times were hard he wrote: ". . . I am resolved to make almost any sacrifice rather than leave old Yarmouth. Her surroundings are part of my existence. I am miserable away from her, her politics, business, men and ways — in general — are as rotten as the Devil can make them. Nevertheless, I'll put up with these if I can only get bread and butter and jog along, somehow."

Arthur Patterson lived in an age when natural history was the hobby of the landed gentry, land-owners, doctors, surgeon, bankers. How frustrated it made him having to work long hours at the warehouse to earn a living wage and how he wished, when he sent in his application in February 1891 for an Attendance Officer's place "I may get it, if so shall feel at greater liberty to pursue natural history work than heretofore." He felt a rich man when his dream came true and he was given the job.

He became a popular speaker at Natural History Societies, Literary Societies, Womens' gatherings and so on. His first talk was given at Acle in 1876.

His talks were popular because they were illustrated. He had the natural gift of storytelling — the kiddies loved his stories and they learned from the simple way he put over his natural history knowledge. "Melinda Twaddles Notions" was written for a bit of fun and the benefit of his fellow townsfolk — it was in a language they could understand. He loved the Norfolk dialect and was proud to be "A Norfolk Dumplin' ". He was pedantic and a stickler for correct names unless "they be rale-broad Norfolk ones" he said.

"June 12th, 1892. Went for a beach, dene and riverside ramble this morning (Sunday). Morning dull. My spirits buoyant (as usual). Everywhere grand. Nature sublime. I could have stopped and kissed the very grass I walked on . . ."

A few weeks later he wrote:

''How I love Nature even to her minutest details — how in quite a different world I seem when I get away from the busy, whirling haunts and ways of men and lose myself in admiring and mixing and drinking in the delights of nature clear away from them.''

He liked solitariness, and in this he was said to resemble the wild things he studied. Someone said ''the life he loved was that he spent alone, or with a congenial companion in his houseboat — beside the wildfowl-frequented Breydon mudflats or in cruising in the ''Yarwhelp'' on the rivers and broads. There he was as much at home as the eel-catcher or smelt-fisher in his ark. Yet there was nothing of a recluse about him for he was always making friends . . .'' He enjoyed the company of fellow naturalists with whom he could share his passion for Nature. Whilst, as he maintained: ''You cannot become a great naturalist by going out with a crowd,'' a naturalist needs to share his experiences with others.

It must have been a disappointment to my great-grandfather that none of his children became naturalists. In August 1889 encouraged at his eldest daughter's interest in fish, he wrote in his diary:

''My little girl aged 8 brought home a Dusky Skulpin which she had picked up on the beach, evidently one cast ashore from a draw net. The little sprite's promised to assist me in things fishy — not a bad start surely . . .''

After that there are few mentions of his family but the children appeared to enjoy walks with their father and he taught the boys to row the punt.

''There had been,'' he wrote, ''a jealous code of fraternity — a newcomer was welcomed very slowly (as is the way of Norfolk folk) and given his position for gunning or picking. One incurred enmity and reprisals when he encroached on another's preserve and he would be kept 'on the books' a twelve-month and get little sport during that time.''

Arthur Patterson gained the confidence of the men who frequented Breydon — even lived like them in a Noah's Ark — and fished alongside them for smelts and picked for eels on the mudflats. He broke down the defences, not only of class but also of the Breydoners and marshmen, whose whole tradition of retinence and secrecy might have led them to regard him as the worst of all possible menaces to their livelihood.

He was always willing to encourage and help others. He befriended the Hunstanton artist Frank Southgate and helped him procure work, and set up a fund for the widow of Charles Harrison. He offered Roland Green accommodation aboard his houseboat and through his sojourn in Broadland he too became a celebrated Broadland artist. When ''Chicko'' Drane, the eel-man, pawned his medals for swimming and lifesaving in 1923, he started a fund to redeem the medals and help the old man ''sit upright.'' Through his newspaper articles and talks, he promoted many charities and supported the public appeal to raise £600 to buy Scolt Head Island for the National Trust.

''Some people,'' he wrote, seem to think I court publicity. I don't, only in one line — naturalistic, but then not for empty reputation; all my endeavour is and has been to make the people believe in and love Nature as I love her.''

''To my biographer. February 1930. It has somewhat amused me when folks of an inquisitive mind have twitted me over MAKING A FORTUNE by book writing and journalism . . . Very few nature writers get back the cost of their productions and the majority lose . . . In my case my books have cost me a big outlay.''

He listed the expenses incurred — three punts, boatshed rents, three houseboats, cost of the "Walrus" cruise, the motor boat trip, repairs, painting and so on over the years.

He admitted to hundreds of outgoings, "namely postage over 40 years — questions asked from the four parts of the compass, parcels of dead birds etc sent which had to be returned or be sent to the British Museum for confirmation of identification, and many tips to persons who brought specimens to my home, paper, ink, pens . . ."

He estimated his expenses to be £237. 10. 0d.

77 With Roland Green, the bird artist near his Mill Studio built on piles driven into the marsh on Hickling Broad, Norfolk. The date was September 18th, 1931 and he and Arthur Patterson were discussing one of the paintings for his London exhibition

Income from Books		£. s. d.
1887	Seaside Scribblings for visitors... Jarrold & Co	£3. 3. 0.
1888	Notes on pet monkeys... L. Upcroft	£17. 0. 0.
1889	Popular Sketches for Sea, Beach and Fireside... Huke	£4. 4. 0.
1889	The Amateur's Zoo... Dean and Son	£5. 0. 0.
1891	Fish Hook and Float... Blake	£2. 2. 0.
1892	Broadland Scribblings... Soman & Co	£12. 0. 0.
1895	Man and Nature on the Broads... Prim. Methodist Pub. Co	£12. 0. 0.
1895	Shadow Entertainments... L. Upcroft p.l.c.	£3. 0. 0.
1901	"Catalogue of Birds" sold privately 100 copies cost £6. 0. 0.	£4. 0. 0.
1903	Life of Charles Harrison, Artist. 175 copies. Presented to Fund what profits made	
1903	From Hayloft to Temple. Got no pay but hawked 200 copies myself	£10. 0. 0.
1904	Notes of an East Coast Naturalist... Methuen roughly	£12. 0. 0.
1905	Nature in Eastern Norfolk... Methuen roughly	£12. 0. 0.
1907	Wildlife on a Norfolk Estuary... Methuen, somewhere about	£12. 0. 0.
1909	Man and Nature on Tidal Waters... Methuen, somewhere about	£12. 0. 0.
1910	Rough Notes on Suffolk Fishes — 111 copies, sold at cost price	
1920	Through Broadland in a Breydon Punt... H. J. Vince — after outlay and incidentals, possibly about	£7. 10. 0.
1923	Cruise of the Walrus on the Broads... Jarrolds after outlay	£7. 10. 0.
1929	Wildfowlers and Poachers... Methuen — to date	£11. 16. 0.
1929	Through Broadland by Sail and Motor... Blake — to date	£15. 0. 0.
1930	In Norfolk Bird Haunts... Rounce & Wortley to date	£5. 10. 0.
		£167. 15. 0d.

Arthur Patterson owed much to Thomas Southwell who "discovered" him and introduced him to the Norfolk and Norwich Naturalists' Society and other eminent naturalists. How humble he must have felt at that first meeting in Norwich when he gave his talk on "Gulls and Terns." He was 32. He said he felt "small and insignificant" and a "dwarf amongst giants" but he had something to offer, and in time he, too, could "hold his head up high."

He labelled himself as "A Common or Garden Field Naturalist" and amongst the books that combined to make him so he listed Gilbert White's "Selborne" and Paget's "Natural History of Great Yarmouth." However, his knowledge came of a lifetime of observation in the "field" and careful, methodical notetaking, which stood him in good stead when writing his books. He was meticulous to detail and a perfectionist. He was well disciplined and always wrote up his diary daily before retiring to bed. He recorded:

"I have occasionally loafed about for hours, returning wet to the skin and chilled through and through, without having seen a gull, crow, or so much as a vagabond wader."

He had patience and used his eyes. He wrote 26 books, numerous pamphlets and articles for periodicals and was a regular contributor to the Eastern Counties Newspapers until his death.

H. E. Hurrell of the Eastern Daily Press said of him: "He was a worthy follower of the Pagets; and as such added to the lists they made of the birds of his native county. He did more, for as an ichthyologist he became a noted authority on Norfolk fishes." He doubled the Yarmouth list and added to the Norfolk list of fishes, shrimps and stalk-eyed crustaceans. He also added to the knowledge of the habits of gulls and waders, as well as rare visitors like the spoonbill and avocet and rediscovered the Old English Black Rat in Yarmouth. Someone said: "He was a veritable mine of information in all matters concerning wildlife" — another "His natural gifts amounted almost to genius."

Edward Jenner, a Lowestoft Naturalist and friend of Arthur Patterson said of him: "Perhaps the best thing he did was to preserve the memory of the old race of Breydoners and other watermen of Yarmouth. In that respect, Yarmouth is more fortunate than Lowestoft. We had in the latter town an equally interesting race of beachmen-fishermen-lifeboatmen now almost all gone, and we have no A.P. to record them for us. In that respect, we envy Yarmouth."

78 Arthur Patterson with abnormal Thornback ray (Raia clavata). The fish was brought in to the fishwharf by Mr. Robert Beezor in July 1922

79 A stone marks the grave of Arthur Patterson and his wife Alice at Gorleston Cemetery next to the Paston family grave

Chapter XXV

John Knowlittle — Great-Grandfather

> "The lives of good, interesting or unique individuals never ought to pass away unnoticed into oblivion."
> A. H. PATTERSON

A hundred people attended my great-grandfather's funeral on October 31st, 1935 at 12 noon at the Primitive Methodist Temple, Great Yarmouth. In recognising his work as a lay preacher, the minister said: "Arthur Patterson was a 'Child of the Temple' whose prayers were the most original heard in the Temple." The congregation sang "O rest in the Lord" and at the closing of the service "Blest are the Departed."

He was buried in my great-grandmother's grave at Gorleston Cemetery. The graveyard, then, was within view of Breydon. He was laid to rest holding his pen —placed there by his son John. Amongst the wreaths lay a spray of wild flowers and plants gathered from his beloved Breydon by young Ted Ellis.

I never knew my great-grandfather but a word-picture by Arthur Smith written in 1901 gives me a clear description:

> "It is easy to picture a wiry, slightly-bowed man, with the profile of an artist of romance, standing where reeds and rushes bow over still waters, intently watching the movements of a rare visitor to Broadland; or to imagine him plodding through a marsh swamp, his hat tilted to the rear and a useful stick tucked under his arm, while he holds a pair of field glasses ready for service. If he has a companion there will be an occasional remark in staccato, a linnet-like movement of the head, or an exchange of opinion regarding the identity of something seen in the distance. Perhaps the swamp gives place to a path by the river, and after a short resting walk on comparatively firm ground, he will cautiously peer over the crest of the river wall, resuming his walk with an Indian growl of discontent, or a brief description of the birds on the mudflats. Perhaps a sturdy marsh farmer, making a detour of his territory, will join him and speak in eloquent broad Norfolk dialect of 'a Spune-bill: a young bahd, wi' no crest to speak of,' which had been seen on Breydon Water, or there may be a discussion regarding the plumage of a hawk seen 'yesterday arternune, out Mautby way.' But any attempt at unimportant small talk is invariably confounded with a curt 'good morning' and Arthur Patterson resumes his walk in the manner of one who must cover within an hour or so, a given number of miles."

He was a handsome man, his face full of character, with distinctive high brow, aquiline features and beard of an artist. His skin, sculptured by the elements, was wrinkled and weatherbeaten. His eyes were brown, bright as a hawk, searching and kindly with a touch of fire and dignity in their glance which drew disciples. He was a quaint, extraordinary personality and, I am told, a cheery companion with a dry, almost sarcastic sense of humour. He was completely unassuming in manner and remained humble all his life in spite of his talents. He was a man who always enjoyed himself, living life to the full and thanking God for each day he passed the age of three score and ten.

80 A photograph by Arthur Smith in September 1905 with friends. With members of the Brown family are Philip Rumbelow, standing behind Patterson, whose diaries aided the research for this book, and seated next to him is life-long friend Ben Dye, who sadly was blind by the time this photograph was taken

The words of a poem by Gerald Bull, I think, describe him well.

THE NATURALIST

"Alone he stands, his step is firm and even;
His hair is comb'd by every wind of heaven,
And shades a brow that juts above keen eyes
Well used to watching where the wonder lies
Of Nature's secret working in the tree,
The plant, the stone, the shell, the bird and bee
Strange life in myriad phases that may hold
His study and his joy till he grow old;
While wood and field his daily steps explore
And add some new discovery to his store.
Serene his state, for he is as a king,
No voice nor law oppose in anything.
While other folk go sad in crowded way,
He thrives alone and lives harmonious days."

Gerald Bull

81 The commemorative tablet of Portland stone at Patterson Close, a thoroughfare in the rebuilt George Street area which the Town Council named after the naturalist. It is within a stone's throw of his birthplace

A multitude of tributes filled the press after great-grandfather's death when he was recognised not only as a writer and naturalist but as an artist, humorist, philosopher and friend.

"To me," wrote Fred Cook, "the passing of A.P. means a great loss and I find it difficult to realise that our friendship has ended — as all good friendships should through death." Arthur Smith said: "He made friends with the lowly and the great and kept their friendship to the last," and "Pedlar" of the "Eastern Daily Press" wrote: ". . . always a lively and entertaining companion with a sense of humour that served him well in his difficult early life, and ensured him a hearty welcome wherever and whenever he was with friends." He left an indelible impression upon all those he met.

Philip Rumbelow, the Yarmouth naturalist whose portrait hangs over the door of the gallery named after him in the Public Library said: "We shall miss him and his work much, not only for what he did but also for the energy he imparted to others." Ted Ellis said: "We record our debt to one who linked young friends with old ones and enriched life for them and inevitably all who come hereafter."

The town of Great Yarmouth honoured John Knowlittle, the Naturalist, in 1957 when they unveiled a tablet in George Street near to where he was born 100 years earlier. It is on one side of Patterson Close in a block of flats named after him. At the Town Hall, old associates of the naturalist recounted their memories of him and spoke in his praise. His son John presented the "Patterson Shield" awarded by the Great Yarmouth Naturalists' Society to thirteen-year-old Janet Spruce of the Priory Girls School, who was adjudged to have kept the best nature notebook during the past year.

Afterwards an exhibition of Patterson relics was on show in the robing room. Ted Ellis gave a radio broadcast about Arthur Patterson's life and one of the art galleries in the Public Library was named in his memory.

They were honouring the boy born 100 years ago in the Rows whose ambition in life had been to write a book on Yarmouth birds. He was the boy who, from an early age, accompanied his father to the allotment near Breydon and was mystified by the queer sounds coming from the estuary. Against parental opposition and extreme poverty he set out to investigate the silver water that lay behind the marsh "walls." He did more than this, for he became an authority on Breydon. Arthur Patterson and Breydon were, in fact, synonymous.

Arthur Patterson's greatest attribute, I think, was not the literature he left us but his ability to impart knowledge and influence others. Just as the Disciples went forth to preach the Word, so does A.P.'s world live on. Ted Ellis was one of the inspiring writers he encouraged so generously and for my entire lifetime his nature column in the "Eastern Daily Press" has "flowed with the ink like a spring from the ground."

I did not experience the company of A.P. but I have through Ted. A walk with him is a delight — it is the way with naturalists. He, like A.P., is a generous, lovable soul, always the same, chatty, informative and helpful. A.P. would be proud of him.

All my great-grandfather's books are out of print, copies are scarce and my fear

82 Presentation of the Patterson Shield, a competition run by the Great Yarmouth Naturalists' Society, to the authoress on October 31st, 1963 by Alderman J. Winter, Mayor

was he was passing away into oblivion. I could not allow that to happen. In a letter to a friend he once wrote: "In my rough and tumble notebooks and in my Diary (undecipherable as it is but always kept up) I usually live knowing I can't be here always and that there may be left something that others may benefit thereby."

John Knowlittle left his notebooks, diaries and literature to Norfolk. Without them I should not have "known" my great-grandfather, and I think I would have liked him.

He was a great philosopher and much of what he said applies today. He strongly opposed wanton spoliation of the Broads and strove for the preservation of wildlife. Though his life was not an easy one he was fortunate to have lived at a time when Broadland was a wildlife paradise. His old heart would grieve today for his beloved Breydon and to see how Broadland has changed.

But his influence lives on and many strive to conserve the Broadland habitat for future naturalists to enjoy, and carry on naturalistic research in which there is no finality. A.P. advised aspiring writers to "keep something in the locker for next time."

Not only is this book the story of a naturalist and his amazing life, it is also a memorial to Breydon and Yarmouth of days gone by. I have barely touched on John Knowlittle's Broadland or his written work. There is, undoubtedly, much left "in the locker" for another time.

BIBLIOGRAPHY

(Based on Norwich Public Library Readers' Guide, Vol. VII, No. 3, July 1918, by George A. Stephen, F.L.A., City Librarian)

BOOKS AND PAMPHLETS

(Arranged chronologically by date of first publication)

1884 Descriptive catalogue of the zoological department of the Preston Pleasure Gardens. Written and compiled for the convenience of visitors [by A. H. Patterson.] Illus., pp. 31. 6⅝ × 4½. Preston: H. Oakey, 1884.

1887 Seaside Scribblings for visitors; or, how to make the most of a holiday jaunt. Illus., pp. 139. 7⅜ × 5. London: Jarrold and Sons, n.d. [1887.]
(Small book containing series of 15 articles on such local celebrities as the beachman, puntgunner, bird catcher, together with chapters "for visitors" which dealt with boating excursions, seaside fishing and other topics.) Reprints from "Yarmouth Gazette," 1885/6.

1888 Notes on pet monkeys and how to manage them. Illus. by F. Lydon, pp. 105. 7¾ × 5. London: L. Upcott Gill, n.d. (1888)
Second (popular) edition. Illus. pp. vi, 98. London: L. Upcott Gill; New York: Charles Scribner's Sons: 1906.
(In preface: "Whatever credit may be deserving is due to Francis Guy, Esq., of Sudbury, at whose instigation I made close acquaintance with quite a colony of monkeys and conceived the idea of scribbling about them.")

1889 Popular Sketches for the sea-beach and fireside. pp. 159. 6½ × 4. Great Yarmouth: A. N. Huke and Co.; London: Simpkin, Marshall and Co., n.d. [1889.]
(Sketches of some of the familiar characters in Yarmouth, followed by a few miscellaneous nature sketches.)

1889 The Amateur's Zoo; or, pet animals, their habits, characteristics, and how to keep and treat them in captivity (Dean's practical guide book). Illus., pp. 110 (ii).7 × 4¾. London: Dean and Son, n.d. [1889.]

1890 Official Guide to Great Yarmouth. Booklet written for competition organised by Town Council Meeting, Gt Yarmouth.

1891 Fish-hook and float: salt water fishing and fresh water angling round about Yarmouth, a book for the visitor angler. Illus., pp. 62. 8¼ × 6½. Great Yarmouth: Stuart C. Blake 1891.
(Contains some line sketches by the author.)

1891 Royal Agricultural Hall, Islington. First appearance in London of the great rorqual whale captured at Great Yarmouth. pp. 8. 6½ × 4. Yarmouth: East Norfolk Printing Co., n.d. [1891]

1892 Broadland Scribblings: a leisure-book for the holidays. By a Broadland naturalist. Illus., pp. (viii), 198. 7⅜ × 4¾. Norwich: P. Soman and Son 1892.
(Sketches of the birds, insects, and fishes of Broadland and some of the well-known characters there.)

1892 A list of the fishes of the Great Yarmouth district; with notes on each species. By "Luberta." Illus., pp. 62. 7¼ × 4⅞. Lowestoft: J. Rochford O'Driscoll, 1892.
(Although "Luberta" was the pseudonym of Mr W. W. Spelman, who issued this book, Mr A. H. Patterson stated that the text was written by him).

1893 Yarmouth Bloater. Pamphlet for the "Perfection Bloater Paste Co. (A. Yallop and Co.)," Great Yarmouth.

1895 Man and Nature on the Broads. Illus., pp. 143. 8¼ × 6¼. London: Thomas Mitchell, n.d. [1895.]
(Sketches, month by month, of the people and bird-life of the Broads. Originally published in the "Primitive Methodist Magazine," 1894.)

1895 Shadow entertainments and how to work them: being something about shadows and the way to make them profitable and funny. Illus., pp. 76. 7¼ × 4¾. London: (Upcott and Gill), n.d. [1895.]

1896 A Protest by a masculine naturalist (Fur, fin and feather leaflets, No. 7: feminine head-gear: the Goura mount.) Illus., pp. 4. 8¾ × 5½. Croydon: Society for the Protection of Birds, 1896.

1896 Rambles in Birdland. Illus., pp. 127. 8¼ × 6½. London: Thomas Mitchell, n.d. [1896.]
(Reprinted from Primitive Methodist Pub. Co. Sketches of the titmouse, robin redbreast, house-sparrow, chaffinch, kingfisher, skylark, blackbird, goldfinch, redstart, swallow, nightingale, golden oriole, song-thrush, common linnet, whitethroat, stonechat, little wren, water wagtail, woodpecker, and bullfinch.

1898 The Mercury Cartoons: A. Patterson's Yarmouth Mercury Cartoons; first series consisting of more than 50, being pen and ink sketches of local interest. Illus., pp. 58. 6½ × 8¾. [Great Yarmouth]: Great Yarmouth Printing Co. 1898.

1898 A souvenir of the Sprat Banquet, Great Yarmouth, 10th December, 1898. Illus., pp. 22. 5 × 8. Great Yarmouth: Jarrold and Sons. 1898. Contains 2 cartoons and a short article on the sprat by Mr. Patterson.

1899 The Mercury Cartoons: Yarmouth Mercury cartoons by A. Patterson; 2nd series of 50. Illus., pp. [54] 6½ × 8¼. [Great Yarmouth:] Great Yarmouth Printing Co. 1899.

1901 Catalogue of the Birds of Great Yarmouth, giving a few descriptive notes, and dates when most of the rarer species were obtained. 12 × illus. pp. (iv), 59. 8½ × 5½. Yarmouth: Great Yarmouth Printing Co. 1901.
(100 copies reprinted from the "Zoologist" (1900) for private circulation. The "catalogue" is preceded by an account of "The Birds of Great Yarmouth and the neighbourhood" (pp. 1-20).

1903 Life of Charles H. Harrison, Broadland Artist. By A. H. Patterson and A. H. Smith. Ports., illus., pp. 60. 8¾ × 5⅝. London: Jarrold and Sons. 1903. (Edition limited to 175 copies.)

1903 From Hayloft to Temple: The story of Primitive Methodism in Yarmouth, biographical, reminiscent, chronological, etc. Ports., illus., pp. xvi, 175. 8¼ × 6¾. London: Robert Bryant 1903.

1904 Notes of an East Coast Naturalist: A series of observations made at odd times during a period of twenty-five years in the neighbourhood of Great Yarmouth; illus. in colour by Frank Southgate, R.B.A., pp. xiii, 304. 8 × 5. London: Methuen and Co. 1904.
(Limited to the fauna of the district. The notes are arranged chronologically. The author states: "It is possible that some of the entries may prove interesting as recording certain traits and habits of the birds and animals of that locality, previously unnoticed by naturalists.")

1905 Nature in Eastern Norfolk. 12 × colour illus. by Frank Southgate, R.B.A. pp. 352.

7 ½ × 5. London: Methuen and Co. 1905.
(Observations on the fauna with a descriptive catalogue of the birds, beasts, and fishes, which occupies the greater part of the book. Has an autobiographical sketch, pp. 1-13).
Second edition. London: Methuen and Co. 1906.

1907 Wildlife on a Norfolk Estuary with preface by Her Grace the Duchess of Bedford. Line illus. by author, pp. xv, 352. London: Methuen and Co. 1907.
(In two portions: (1) Nature notes, chiefly on bird-life on Breydon; and (2) East Coast notes, in continuation of the author's "Notes of an East Coast Naturalist".)

1909 Man and Nature on tidal waters. Ports., illus., pp. xvi, 315. 7 ½ × 5. London: Methuen and Co. 1909.
(Sketches of the wild-life of Breydon and its neighbourhood. Contents: In wintry days. On guns and gunners. "Public" affairs. Shallow waters. Shrimpers and shrimping. With the eel fishers. On quiet waters. Some lost industries. Dead low water. Harvest of the sea. Flotsam.)

1910 Rough notes on the fish and fisheries of East Suffolk. Illus. by author, pp. (vi), 55. 8 ½ × 5. Great Yarmouth: John Buckle 1910.
(111 copies reprinted from the "Zoologist" (1909) for private circulation with 14 illustrations and a map by the author).

1912 A souvenir commemorating my twenty years' work as an attendance officer. Illus., pp. 15. 6 ¼ × 10. Great Yarmouth: J. Buckle, printer. [1912].
(100 copies printed for private circulation. A series of cartoons, with prefatory page of text, dated November 1912.)

1920 Through Broadland in a Breydon Punt by John Knowlittle (A.H.P.). Illus., pp. xvi, 112. Norwich: H. J. Vince (1920) with preface by G. Christopher Davies.
(Reprinted from "Eastern Daily Press", autumn 1919)

1923 The Cruise of the "Walrus" on the Broads: a Broadland Voyage in a North-sea Ketch-boat. Preface by Walter Rye. Illus., pp. 175. London: Jarrolds Publishers (London) Ltd. (1923).

1929 Wild-fowlers and poachers: fifty years on the East Coast. Illus. 25 by author, 12 other, end-paper map. pp. xiv, 284. London: Methuen and Co. Ltd. 1929.

1930 A Norfolk Naturalist: observations on birds, mammals and fishes. Illus. 35 by author and a frontispiece from painting of Charles H. Harrison. pp. xii, 209. London: Methuen and Co. Ltd. 1930.

1930 Through Broadland by sail and motor. Port., illus., pen and ink drawings by author, pp. vi., 141. London: Blakes Limited 1930.

1930 In Norfolk Bird Haunts in A.D.1755. Reprinted from the "Norfolk Chronicle" Series. Illus. with pen and ink sketches by the author, pp. 103. Holt, Norfolk: Rounce and Wortley (1930).

ARTICLES

Abbreviations:
N.N.N.S. = Transactions of the Norfolk & Norwich Naturalists' Society.
Zool. = The Zoologist.

1878 First published natural history paragraph in the shape of a letter, September 19th. In "Standard," 1878.
Second published nature letter on late swallows. In "Eastern Daily Press," November 18th, 1878.
Subsequent natural history articles and letters in "Eastern Daily Press" and other publications chronologically inserted in notebooks 1878-1935 in custody of Norfolk Record Office.

1880 Bird Notes of a Young Naturalist. In "Yarmouth Chronicle." 1880.

1881 Scribblings of a Naturalist by "Rambler." In "Yarmouth Mercury." 1881.
Natural History articles. In "Yarmouth Independent." 1881.
Natural History articles. In "Bazaar, Exchange and Mart," 1881.
Articles condemning collecting birds eggs. In "Yarmouth Chronicle," 1881.

1885 Local Celebrities of Gt. Yarmouth. In "Yarmouth Gazette," 1885.
(See Books and Pamphlets)

1886 Chapters for Visitors. In "Yarmouth Gazette," 1886.
(See Books and Pamphlets)
Notes on Pet Monkeys. Articles in ? London periodical, 1886.

1889 A Chapter for the Little Folks. In "Yarmouth Gazette," 1889.
Articles. In "Naturalists Gazette," 1889.

1890-3 A Rare Fish. In "Field Club (a magazine of general natural history for scientific and unscientific readers)" ed. by Rev. Theodore Wood, F.E.S., vol. 4, pp. 92-93. Elliot Stock 1890-3.

1891 Notes on some rare sea-fishes, found in the neighbourhood of Gt. Yarmouth. In "N.N.N.S.," Vol. 5, 1894, pp. 227-30.
Rare Birds. First contribution to "Zoologist." April 14th, 1891.
Article for "Natural History Society" for which he won first prize. November 1891.

1892 Some marine notes from Yarmouth. In "N.N.N.S.," Vol. 5, 1894, pp. 323-328.

1892-3 The fishes of East Anglia. In "Eastern Daily Press," August 29th, 1892-January 14th, 1893. A series of 60 articles on fishes.

1892-4 Pets worth keeping. In "Bazaar, Exchange and Mart." The title of a series of articles. 1892-4. London: L. Upcott Gill.

1892-8 Short notes from a naturalist's notebook. In diary form in "Gt. Yarmouth Annual," 1892-8.

1893-1931 Melinda Twaddles' Notions. A weekly article in dialect in "Yarmouth Mercury." 1893-April 1931.

1893-4 Chapters for Young Naturalists. Illus. In "Springtime (monthly magazine)". London: Primitive Methodist Pub. Co. pp. 6-9, 40-43, 73-75, 104-107,

152-156, 177-181, 214-217, 245-249, 269-271, 277-281, 302-305, 345-348, 370-372.
pp. 11-15, 44-49, 79-83, 112-116, 146-149, 176-178, 208-212, 242-245, 279-284, 301-304, 329-334, 364-366.
(See Books and pamphlets)

1893 Natural History of the months. Illus. In "Aldersgate Magazine." 1893 vol. 74 (new series, vol. 16) pp. 33-35, 101-105, 163-166, 216-219, 277-281, 345-348, 422-424, 471-474, 533-537, 602-605, 681-684, 737-741. London: Primitive Methodist Pub. Co.
(See Books and pamphlets)

1894-99 Some odd notes from a naturalist's diary. In "East Norfolk Annual," 1894, pp. 105-111; 1895, pp. 105-113; 1896, pp. 105-113; 1897, pp. 133-141; 1898, pp. 97-113; 1899, pp. 97-109.

1895 Some marine notes from Yarmouth. In "N.N.N.S.," vol. 6, 1899. pp. 114-117.

1896 Fish notes from Yarmouth. In "N.N.N.S.," vol. 6, 1899, pp. 225-227.
The Drawing Room: Lightning Cartoons. In "Bazaar, Exchange and Mart, 1896.
From the Log of the Moorhen. In "Eastern Daily Press." 1896.

1897 From the Log of the Moorhen. In "Eastern Daily Press." August/September 1897.

1897-1916 Annual Report on Norfolk Fishes. In "Zool.," 1897-1916.

1897 Broadland Sketches (Sunday snapshots). Chapters in "Aldersgate Magazine," new series, vol. 4.
Service at Reedly Chapel: a Broadland Sketch. pp. 196-200.
Snapshots in the Broadlands, II. Sunday School Anniversary at Pikely. pp. 374-8.
Sunday afternoon at Easter: a Broadland Sketch. pp. 441-4.
At Lilyford Love-feast. pp. 523-7.
Sedgehampton Campmeeting. pp. 601-606.
Snapshots in the Broadlands: Rushfield Harvest Festival. pp. 762-7.
Snapshots in the Broadlands: Fenbrook Mission Services. pp. 902-7.
London: Primitive Methodist Pub. Co. 1897.

1897-1914 Natural History Notes from Yarmouth. In N.N.N.S.," vol. 6, 1899, pp. 291-5, 405-8, 484-8; vol. 7, 1904, pp. 63-71, 177-184, 395-400, 566-571, 726-730; vol. 8, 1909. pp. 111-116, 315-322, 460-77, 604-15, 755-762; vol. 9, 1914, pp. 79-89, 193-7, 455-8.

1898 Snapshots in the Broadlands: weeknight service at Ruddpool. Chapter in "Aldersgate Magazine," new series, vol. 5, 1898, pp. 97-101.
Where two or three are gathered together. pp. 289-292.
Service at Holmsby Warren: A Broadland Sketch. pp. 681-5.

1900 Yarmouth in 1909: a prophesy. In "Gt. Yarmouth Printing Co.'s Annual," 1900, pp. 109-135.

1901 The Caister Lifeboat Disaster. Cover picture for "Supplement to Yarmouth Mercury." November 18th, 1901. Gt. Yarmouth Printing Co. Ltd.

1901 From the Log of the "Moorhen." In "The Naturalists' Journal," vol. 10, 1901. pp. 20-25, 37-41, 55-59, 75-80, 93-97, 111-115, 131-133, 149-153. Huddersfield.

1901 Yarmouth 100 years ago. In "Yarmouth Independent." 1901.

1902 History of Primitive Methodism at Gt. Yarmouth and the Circuit. Christmas 1902. In Primitive Publishing Co. magazine.

Punctuality. An article for Primitive Methodist Improvement Society, Gt. Yarmouth.

John Thomas, punt gunner. In "N.N.N.S.," vol. 7, 1904, pp. 339-345.

1902(?) Icebound near home: an old man's yarn of Breydon. In "The Gt. Yarmouth Printing Co's. Annual," 1902(?), pp. 129-137.

1903 Snob-shop gossip. In "The Gt. Yarmouth Printing Co's. Annual," 1903. pp. 129-141.

Some Broadland topics: an old man's yarn of the Broads. In "The Gt. Yarmouth Printing Co's. Annual," 1903, pp. 113-123.

Wild life on Breydon. In William A. Dutt's "The Norfolk Broads, a Guide to", 1903, pp. 200-214.

Articles on animals. In "Primitive Methodist Magazine," 1903.

Mollusca of Gt. Yarmouth District. In "Zool.," 1903.

Scotch articles. In "Norwich Mercury," October to November 1903.

1904 David Garrod's yarns. In "The Gt. Yarmouth Printing Co.'s Annual," 1904, pp. 99-107.

1904-16 Some fish-notes from Gt. Yarmouth. In "Zool.," 4th ser., vol. 8, 1904, pp. 441-4; vol. 9, 1905, pp. 441-6; vol. 10, 1906, pp. 453-8; vol. 11, 1907, pp. 460-4; vol. 12, 1908, pp. 441-9; vol. 14, 1910, pp. 63-8, 451-61; vol. 15, 1911, pp. 11-13, 441-9; vol. 16, 1912, pp. 29-32; vol. 17, 1913, pp. 15-32; vol. 18, 1914, pp. 1-20; vol. 19, 1915, pp. 1-20; vol. 20, 1916, pp. 1-21. Series of annual notes. In 1914 the words "and the neighbourhood" were added to the title.

1905 A gossip of some Yarmouth Fishes. In "The Gt. Yarmouth Printing Co.'s Annual," 1905, pp. 83-95.

Among Norfolk Terns. In "Zool.," 4th ser. vol. 9, 1905, pp. 258-62.

On a Norfolk Heronry. In "Zool.," 4th ser. vol. 9, 1905, pp. 301-306.

A Sunday on Breydon. In "Zool.," 4th ser. vol. 9, 1905, pp. 367-75.

Reminiscences of Breydon. In "The Gt. Yarmouth Printing Co.'s Annual," 1905, pp. 107-115.

The Making of a Naturalist. In "The Countryside," 1905.

1906 Some Crustacean gossip from Gt. Yarmouth. In "Zool.," 4th ser., vol. 10, 1906, pp. 331-4.

1907 Birds and the Great Snow. In "Zool.," 4th ser., vol. 11, 1907, pp. 81-91.

Some holiday notes from Breydon. In "Zool.," 4th ser., vol. 11, 1907, pp. 361-66.

Birdwatching in a Breydon punt; August in a Breydon punt; An October east-coast ramble; In east Norfolk bird haunts. In "The book of the Open air. British Country Life in Spring and Summer," edited by Edward Thomas. Illus. vol. 1, pp. 56-63, 175-183; vol. 2, 41-49, 107-120. London: Hodder and Stoughton, 1907.

1907-8 Notes on pet Wildfowl. By "Nature Lover." In "Bazaar, Exchange and Mart," 1907-8. A monograph on the subject of wildfowl keeping in captivity, about 20,000 words.

1908 The Badger in Norfolk. In "Zool.," 4th ser., vol. 12, 1908, pp. 426-7.

Some mud-flat bird-notes. In "Zool.," 4th ser., vol. 13, 1908, pp. 208-12.

1909 Rough notes on the fish and fisheries of East Suffolk. In "Zool.," 4th ser., vol. 13, 1909, pp. 361-392, 414-421, 447-462.
Fauna and flora of Norfolk; additions to parts iv., fishes. In "N.N.N.S.," vol. 8, 1909, pp. 844-847.
Notes on a decayed trawl-fishery. In "N.N.N.S.," vol. 9, 1914, pp. 26-42.

1910-14 Chats about the birdies. Chapters for Young Naturalists. In "Springtime," 1910-14. Primitive Methodist Pub. Co.

1911 Scribblings of a naturalist. In "Aldersgate Magazine," 12 chapters, 1911. Primitive Methodist Pub. Co.
Notes on the whales of Norfolk. In "N.N.N.S.," vol. 9, 1914, pp. 300-7.
Some odd notes on Yarmouth fishes. In "Zool.," 4th ser., vol. 15, 1911, pp. 219-225.
The Codling Invasion. In "Anglers' News.," Feb. 11th, 1911.

1912 Some miscellaneous notes from Gt. Yarmouth. In "Zool.," 4th ser., vol. 16, 1912, pp. 417-423.

1913 Some miscellaneous notes from Gt. Yarmouth (1913). In "Zool.," 4th ser., vol. 17, 1913, pp. 361-369.

1914 Some miscellaneous notes from Gt. Yarmouth (1913-14). In "Zool.," 4th ser., vol. 18, 1914, pp. 375-392.
Fauna and flora of Norfolk: additions to part iv., fishes. In "N.N.N.S.," vol. 9, 1914, pp. 815-821.
Some nature pages. In "The English Year," edited by W. Beach Thomas and A. K. Collett. London: T. C. and E. C. Jack, 1914. Contains a few unsigned articles by A. H. Patterson and some of his sketches. Spring volume, pp. 70-77, pp. 209-214; Summer volume, pp. 319-325; Autumn and winter volume, pp.181-183, 328-335, 352-362.

1914 Nature around Lowestoft. Lowestoft Souvenir of the Conference of the National Union of Teachers, pp. 109-114, Jarrold and Sons Ltd., Easter 1914.

1915 Some miscellaneous notes from Yarmouth, (1914-15). In "Zool.," 4th ser., vol. 19, 1915, pp. 361-375.
Some ornithological war-notes from Gt. Yarmouth. In "Zool.," 4th ser., vol. 19, 1915, pp. 93-97.

1916 Some miscellaneous notes from Gt. Yarmouth (1915-16). In "Zool.," 4th ser., vol. 20, 1916, pp. 361-377.
The "Zoologist" was disbanded in January 1917.
The January flood of 1916 at Gt. Yarmouth. In "N.N.N.S.," vol. 10, pp. 162-167.
The Yarmouth herring fishery of 1915. In "N.N.N.S.," vol. 10, pp. 174-176.

1917 Some fish-notes from Gt. Yarmouth and neighbourhood for 1916. In "N.N.N.S.," vol. 10, pp. 213-231.

1918 Yarmouth Herring Fishery of 1917. In "N.N.N.S.," vol. 10, pp. 361-366.
Yarmouth Bird Notes, 1917. In "N.N.N.S.," vol. 10, pp. 367-70.
Yarmouth Fish Notes, 1917. In "N.N.N.S.," vol. 10, pp. 371-80.

1919 Through Broadland in a Breydon Punt. 18 chapters. In "Eastern Daily Press," July to August 1919.
The late Frank Norgate. In "British Birds," 1919.
The Herring Fishery of 1918. In "N.N.N.S.," vol. 10, pp. 487-490.
Some Fish Notes for 1918 from Gt. Yarmouth and neighbourhood. In

"N.N.N.S.," vol. 10, pp. 490-493.
Some bird notes for 1918 from Gt. Yarmouth. In "N.N.N.S.," vol. 10, pp. 494-498.
Common Rorqual off the East Coast. In "N.N.N.S.," vol. 10, pp. 505-506.
1920 A Naturalist's Tramp round the Norfolk Coast. In "Eastern Daily Press," 9 chapters. August, 1920.
The Herring Fishery of 1919. In "N.N.N.S.," vol. 11, pp. 204-5.
1921 Holiday Nights and Days on Breydon. In "Norwich Mercury Series," 12 chapters. July 28-September, 1921.
Nature articles. In "Natureland," 1921.
1922 The Herring Fishery of 1921. In "N.N.N.S.," vol. 11, pp. 314-315.
Fishnotes from Gt. Yarmouth. In "Natureland," vol. 11, No. 4, 4 pp. (15); vol. 11, No. 3.
1923 Schooldays in the Sixties. Death of William Wallis. In "Eastern Daily Press," Dec. 22nd, 1923.
Sketches by John Knowlittle. In "Carrow Works Magazine," 1923.
1924-25 The Herring Fishery of 1923. In "N.N.N.S.," vol. 12, part 1, p. 114.
The Herring Fishery of 1924. In "N.N.N.S.," vol. 12, part 1, p. 117.
Miscellaneous Notes and Observations: White beaked dolphin; Melanistic Common Rat; Norfolk Summer Woodcock. In "N.N.N.S.," vol. 12, part 1, p. 128.
1925 Big shots by the old Breydon gunners. In "Country Life," April 4th, 1925, (vol. 57, No. 1474) p. 61.
1925? Brundall on the Broads: An ideal River Trip. Presented by The Brundall Gardens Steamship Co. Ltd. 1925?
1925-6 The Herring Fishery of 1925. In "N.N.N.S.," vol. 12, part 2, p. 184.
1926 Observations. In "British Birds," edited by H. F. Witherby. 1926.
1926-7 Bird Notes. In "N.N.N.S.," vol. 12, part 3, 1924-6, p. 199.
The Herring Fishery of 1926. In "N.N.N.S.," vol. 12, part 3, p. 303.
Miscellaneous Notes and Observations: Albino Rats; Abnormal Skate; Food of the Sturgeon. In "N.N.N.S.," vol. 12, part 3, p. 380.
1927 Recollections of life in the Sixties and Seventies. In "Yarmouth Mercury" and "Eastern Daily Press." 1927.
1927-8 The Herring Fishery of 1927. In "N.N.N.S.," vol. 12, part 4, p. 475.
Miscellaneous Notes and Observations: Crossbills; Ray's Bream; Rorqual Whale; and Food of the Herring. In "N.N.N.S.," vol. 12, part 4, p. 525.
1927-30 A Naturalist's Notebook by "Broadlander." In "The Anglers' News." 1927-30.
1928 Life's little humours. In "Bric-a-brac (a small magazine issued for Yarmouth Hospital Day)". Illus. August 9th, 1928.
1929 Topical Remembrances. In "Eastern Daily Press." 1929.
1930 A sketch by John Knowlittle included Mustard Pot. In "Carrow Works Magazine," 1930.
Wildlife on Breydon, by Arthur Patterson. Wildfowling, by Nicholas Everitt and A. H. Patterson. Fishes, by A. H. Patterson. In W. A. Dutt's "The Norfolk Broads." 1930. pp. 195-216, 339-349, 387-393.
1931 Nature Notes. Illus. In "Yarmouth Mercury." 1931.
Some Yarmouthian nature-gossip; Some reminiscences of a school attendance

officer. In "Souvenir of the National Union of Teachers conference, Gt. Yarmouth." Easter 1931. Illus. pp. 28-32. Jarrold and Sons Ltd.

A Breydonian Quartette in Bonnie Springtime, by John Knowlittle. In "Snapdragon," in aid of hospital. Christmas 1931. pp. 4. 10,000 copies sold.

1933 Some old Yarmouth Sportsmen. In "Yarmouth Mercury." 29 articles. 1933.

Frontispiece by Arthur Patterson. In "From Stickleback to Salmon, 50 years of fishing. All Truth and no Lies," by F. W. Goodness, M.P.S. Jarrold and Sons Ltd. 1933.

1934 Bits of old-time Yarmouth. Series of articles recalling his childhood and youth. In "Yarmouth Mercury." 1934.

CARTOONS

(See also section on Books and pamphlets, 1898 and 1899)

1892 Election cartoons, black and white, for display in window of Yarmouth Office of "Eastern Daily Press."

1897-1914 "Yarmouth Mercury" Cartoons. 7 vols.
These volumes contain about 1,000 of Arthur Patterson's cartoons relating to local politics and events, which he contributed to the "Yarmouth Mercury." Commenced 21st September 1897.
1st series of 50 reprinted in book form in 1898.
2nd series of 50 reprinted in book form in 1899.

1901 "Moral Sermons" or proverbs. A series of coloured cartoons for display in "Eastern Daily Press" Yarmouth Office window.

1902 Humours of Norfolk History. A series of 60 cartoons in "Yarmouth and Gorleston Times." December 6th, 1902.

1903 Football cartoons by "Broadlander" in "Eastern Evening News" September 15th, 1903 to April 1906.

1914 Humours of Angling. In "The Angler's News and Sea Fisher's Journal," Feb. 28, March 14, 28, April 11, 25, May 9, 23, June 6, 27, July 11, 25, Aug. 8, 22, Sept. 5, 19, and October 3, 1914.